CHARLES PÉGUY

THE MYSTERY OF THE CHARITY OF

JOAN OF ARC

TRANSLATED BY JULIAN GREEN

PANTHEON

Printed in the United States of America
by Belgrave Press, Inc.

FOREWORD

Charles Péguy is among the very few French authors whose work calls for something like a literal translation. His idea of style is extremely peculiar and his language is his very own. Not very long ago, I was talking with the Catholic novelist François Mauriac, who is well known in Paris for his quick and witty retorts, and he asked me what I was writing. I said that I was finishing a translation of Péguy into English, whereupon, with a toss of the head, he exclaimed: "What a pity someone doesn't try to translate him into French!" This is, of course, unfair, but any reader of Péguy will understand what Mauriac meant.

In rereading his Mystère de la Charité de Jeanne d'Arc, *I was struck by the extraordinary importance Péguy gives each word in this poem, and not each word only, but each typographical sign down to the last comma. It is as if the very letters he uses were so many messengers to whom an all-important communication had been entrusted. No one that I know in French literature has ever had a greater appreciation of the values of written speech and in his speech as in his life, Péguy was the Frenchest of the French. For that reason, to give an English equivalent of his style is, I believe, almost impossible. No Englishman ever spoke like Joan of Arc or Madame Gervaise in the translation which I have just brought to an end, but I should also make it very plain that no French-*

5

man ever wrote like Péguy, although the man in the streets of Paris or Orléans is apt to speak exactly as Péguy wrote, particularly if he is in an argumentative mood, particularly if he likes words. Few men ever loved words quite so much as Péguy, and by words I mean spoken words, all the words people squander with such reckless extravagance all day long. Péguy was full of words, but he was also full of inspiration. His books are spoken rather than written and lack something of their meaning if they are not read aloud. The strange thing about Péguy's inspiration is that it never makes him lose his head: he speaks with tremendous force and inner conviction, but he is never feverish. His speech is abundant, yet never precipitate. His patience is inexhaustible when it comes to proving a point and he does so with such thoroughness that when the question is settled, it is settled, as he would put it in his own Péguy-French, eternally forever.

That he loved the French language is beyond doubt, but he took what then seemed outrageous liberties with it. When the language refused to say what Péguy wanted, he made it. Grammar shrieked with pain, but there you are: the language is grateful today for the violence it suffered at the hands of this muscular poet, and modern French would not be quite what it is now if that "considerable passer-by" (as Mallarmé called Rimbaud) had not marched into the twentieth century with his heavy boots, his beard and that unbecoming pince-nez of his.

My purpose was not, of course, to imitate Péguy's style in English, but to follow it as closely and as scrupulously as possible in the hope that I could perhaps give a correct impression of the original. When the translator's grammar seems wild, I beg the reader to glance at the French and see if Péguy's isn't wilder. It may be said that this translation does not sound like English. I shall be very gratified if it doesn't. I am not so interested in hav-

6

ing it sound like English as I am in having it sound like Péguy.

I may add that I have almost always used his own peculiar punctuation. In a few places, however, I have squeezed in commas which would no doubt have put him in a rage, but the reader may feel that I was right.

Where Péguy writes "Mon Dieu," and he writes it often, I have written "Lord." Somehow it sounds nearer to "Mon Dieu" than "My God." And quieter.

Finally, the reader may be interested to know that, according to Romain Rolland in his book on Charles Péguy, Madame Gervaise who has so much to say to Joan of Arc and so much to teach her, is a symbolical figure personifying the Church. This seems likely enough in certain speeches, although Péguy, to my knowledge, never made it clear. It may be well, also, to remember that this poem is not an account of Joan of Arc's life, but rather an attempt to describe the awakening of her supernatural vocation.

JULIAN GREEN

THE MYSTERY
OF THE CHARITY OF
JOAN OF ARC

Morning. Jeannette, the daughter of Jacques d'Arc, spins as she tends her father's sheep, on a hillside by the Meuse River.

From right to left, in the background, the Meuse is seen flowing through meadows, also the village of Domremy with the church, and the road leading to Vaucouleurs.

To the left, in the distance, the village of Maxey.

Hills in the background; facing the spectator, wheat fields, vineyards and woods; the wheat fields are yellow.

Jeannette is thirteen and a half; Hauviette, her friend, a few months over ten.

Madame Gervaise is twenty-five.

(Jeannette goes on spinning; then she rises; turns toward the church; says the sign of the cross without making it.)

JEANNETTE

In the name of the Father; and of the Son; and of the
Holy Ghost; Amen.

Our Father who art in heaven; hallowed be thy
name; thy kingdom come; thy will be done on earth
as it is in heaven; give us this day our daily bread;
forgive us our trespasses as we forgive those who trespass against us; and lead us not into temptation; but
deliver us from evil. Amen.

Hail Mary, full of grace, the Lord is with thee;
blessed art thou amongst women; and blessed is the
fruit of thy womb Jesus. Holy Mary, mother of God,
pray for us sinners, now and at the hour of our death.
Amen.

Saint John, my patron saint; Saint Joan, my patron
saint, pray for us; pray for us.

In the name of the Father; and of the Son; and of the
Holy Ghost. Amen.

Our father, our father who art in heaven, how far
is your name from being hallowed; how far is your
kingdom from coming.

Our father, our father who art in the kingdom of
heaven, how far is your kingdom from coming to the
kingdom of the earth.

Our father, our father who art in the kingdom of
heaven, how far is your kingdom from coming to the
kingdom of France.

Our father, our father who art in heaven, how far is your will from being done; how far are we from being given our daily bread.

How far are we from forgiving those who trespass against us; and not succumbing to temptation; and being delivered from evil. Amen.

O God, if we could only see the beginning of your kingdom. If we could only see the sun of your kingdom rise. But there is nothing, there is never anything. You have sent us your son whom you loved so dearly, your son came, who suffered so much, and died. And now, nothing. There is never anything. If we could only see the daybreak of your kingdom. And you have sent us your saints, you have called each one of them by his name, your other sons the saints and your daughters the saints, and your saints have come, men and women, and now, nothing, there is never anything. Years have gone by, so many years that I cannot count them; centuries of years have gone by; fourteen centuries of Christianity, alas, since the nativity, and the death, and the preaching. And now, nothing, nothing, ever. And what reigns on the face of the earth is nothing, nothing, is nothing but perdition. Fourteen centuries (but were they Christian centuries?), fourteen centuries since the redemption of our souls. And nothing, nothing, ever, the reign of the earth is nothing but the reign of perdition, the kingdom of the earth is nothing but the kingdom of perdition. You have sent us your son and the other saints. And nothing flows down upon the face of the earth but a stream of ingratitude and perdition. God, God, will it have to be that your son died in vain? That he should have come and come in vain? It is worse than ever. Only, if we could only see the sun of your justice rise. But it looks as if, God, God, forgive me, it looks as if your reign were passing away. Never has your name been so blasphemed. Never has your will been so despised. Never has there been such disobedience. Never have we so much lacked our bread; and if we were the only ones to lack it, God, if we were the only ones; and if it were only the bread of the body which we lacked, the corn bread, the rye and wheat bread; but there is another bread which we lack, the bread for the nourishment of our souls; and we are hungry with another hunger, with the only hunger which leaves an everlasting hollow in our stomachs. There is another bread which we lack. And instead of the reign of your charity, the only reign reigning on the face of the earth, the earth of your creation, instead of the reign of the kingdom of your charity, we have the reign of the imperishable kingdom of sin. If we could at least see the beginning of your saints, if we could see the dawn of the beginning of this reign of your saints. But, God, what have they done, what have they done with your creature, what have they done with your creation? Never have so many trespassed and never has so much trespassing died unforgiven. Never has Christian trespassed so much against Christian, and against you, God, never has man trespassed so much against you. And never has so much trespassing died unforgiven. Will it be said that you have sent us your son in vain, and that your son has suffered in vain, and that he has died. And will it have to be in vain that he sacrifices himself and that we sacrifice him every day. What have they done with the Christian people, God, what have they done with your people. And not only do temptations besiege us, but temptations triumph, and temptations reign, and it is the reign of temptation, and the reign of the kingdoms of the earth has altogether fallen into the reign of the kingdom of temptation, and the evil succumb to the temptation of evil, the temptation to do evil, to do evil to others, and, God, forgive me, to do evil to you; but the good, who were good, succumb to a temptation infinitely worse: the temptation to believe that they have been forsaken by you. In the name of the Father, and of the Son, and of the Holy Ghost, Lord, deliver us from evil, deliver us from evil. If there have not yet been enough saints, men and women, send us some more, send us as many as will be needed, send us so many that the enemy will get tired. We will follow them, God. We will do everything you wish. We will do everything they wish. We will do everything they tell us in your name. We are your faithful, send us your saints; we are your sheep, send us your shepherds; we are the flock, send us the pastors. We are good Christians, you know that we are good Christians. So how is it that so many good Christians don't make up a good Christendom. There must be something wrong. If you could send us, if only you would send us one of your holy women. There are still some. People say that there are. Some have been seen. Some are heard of. Some are known. But we don't know how it is managed. There are saints among women, there is holiness and never did the reign of the kingdom of perdition so entirely dominate the face of the earth. Perhaps something else is needed, Lord, you know everything. You know what we lack. Perhaps we need something new, something no one has ever seen. Something no one has ever done. But who would dare say, Lord, that there could be anything new after fourteen centuries of Christianity, after so many saints, men and women, after all your martyrs, after the passion and death of your son.

(She sits down and resumes her spinning.)

What we need, God, what we finally need is a woman who would also be a saint . . . and who would succeed.

(A voice rises from the valley, coming closer. It is Hauviette. She comes up by the path from the market town, and sings.)

Never shall in English power
Fall good Saint Nicholas' tower.

JEANNETTE

Lord, Lord, we will really be good, we will be dutiful, we will be obedient. We will be faithful.

Lord, Lord, we are your children, we are your children.

(Hauviette appears.)

Lord, Lord, what have they made of your people.

(Enter Hauviette. She begins, half talking, half singing, as if her words were a natural sequel to her song and only by degrees does she come down to her ordinary way of speaking.)

HAUVIETTE

How do you do, Jeannette.

JEANNETTE

How do you do, Hauviette.

(A pause.)

HAUVIETTE

You were saying your prayers?

JEANNETTE

(A rather long pause.)

I was. There is such a lack. There is much to ask for.

HAUVIETTE

The good Lord knows what we need, the good Lord knows what we lack.

(Still in a chattering sort of way.)

You were saying your prayers. Don't apologize about it. Don't deny it. I am not blaming you. You don't have to deny it. There is no harm in it. You needn't feel ashamed.

JEANNETTE

(A pause.)

I was saying my prayers. You too, Hauviette, you say your prayers.

HAUVIETTE

I am a good Christian like every one else, I say my prayers like everyone else, I am a good parishioner like every one else. Eh? I say my prayers morning and evening, *Our Father* and *Hail Mary* to begin my day

15

and end it up. And that fills up my day. Eh? That's enough to fill up my day, it holds my day together; it keeps my heart steady all day. It makes me pass the whole day. I am a good Christian. You say your two prayers just as you eat your three meals. It is just as natural. It's the same thing. It's what makes up the day. You don't eat all day long. You don't say your prayers all day long. I am a good parishioner. I also say my prayers at the morning *Angelus* and at the evening *Angelus,* no matter what I may be doing, I stop doing it, of course, to pray as the church bell rings. I am a good parishioner of the parish of Domremy. I go to catechism like everyone else. And on Sunday, I go to town for mass and to church like everyone else. But there you are, me, I don't want Sunday to be like the other days of the week and the days of the week to be like Sunday. And the hours given up to prayer to be like the other hours of the day, and the other hours of the day to be like the hours of prayer. Or else, then, otherwise, it will be as if there weren't any Sunday. During the week. And no hours of prayer. During the day. So it's no use having Sunday. You mustn't work on Sunday. But you've got to work on week days. There is a day for the good Lord and the other days are meant for work. To work is to pray. I got to catechism Sunday morning before mass. There is a time for everything. Sufficient unto the hour is the evil thereof. And its task. Each thing in its time. To work, to pray, it's quite natural, it takes care of itself.

Sunday must stand out in the week and the *Angelus* and the hour of prayer must stand out in the day.

Yes indeed, Jeannette, my fine girl, I say my prayers, but you are never done saying yours, you say them all the time, you are never done with them, you say them at all the roadside crosses, the church isn't enough for you. Never have the roadside crosses been used so much . . .

JEANNETTE

Hauviette, Hauviette.

HAUVIETTE

Don't lose your temper, my fine one. Never have the roadside crosses been used so much.

JEANNETTE

Alas, alas one cross was used one day, a real cross made of wood, on a mountain, was used once upon a time . . . and what a time.

HAUVIETTE

You see, you see. What we know, we girls, you see it. What we are taught, we girls, you see it. The catechism, the whole catechism, and the church, and mass, you don't know these things, you see them, and your prayers, you don't say them, you don't say them only, you see them. For you there are no weeks. And there are no days. There are no days in the week, and no hours in the day. Every hour that strikes is like the *Angelus* bell for you. Every day is Sunday and more than Sunday, and Sunday more than Sunday and than Christmas Sunday and than Easter Sunday and mass more than mass . . .

JEANNETTE

There is nothing that is more than mass.

HAUVIETTE

I am a good parishioner of the parish of Domremy in Lorraine, in my Lorraine of Christendom. So there. That's all. But as for you, never had the crosses of this country served so much since you came into the world, never had the crosses served so much, never had the crosses of Christendom in these parts, the crosses of this country of Christendom received so many prayers, all the time since they came into the world, as they have done for the thirteen years and a half since you yourself came into the world. That's what I know. And so does the cross that stands at the crossing of the road to Maxey.

JEANNETTE

Alas, alas, that is the road that leads to the enemy, the road to the enemy town. How can Christians be enemies, children of the same God, brothers of Jesus.

All of them brothers of Jesus.

HAUVIETTE

So much so that you are ashamed . . .

JEANNETTE

Hauviette, Hauviette.

HAUVIETTE

So much so that you are ashamed of always being at prayers and that you hide. You say the sign of the cross instead of making it, at the beginning and at the end of your prayers, so you won't be seen, because you'd be doing it all the time.

JEANNETTE

Alas.

HAUVIETTE

You want to be like the others. You want to be like everyone else. You don't want to be noticed. Try as you may. You'll never succeed.

JEANNETTE

I am a shepherdess like every one else, I am a Christian like every one else, I am a parishioner like every one else.

I am your friend and I am like yourself.

HAUVIETTE

Try as you may, talk as much as you please, believe as much as you please: you are our friend, but you will never be like us.

I don't hold it against you. I am in the good Lord's hand. We are in the good Lord's hand, all of us, and the earth, the whole of it, is in the good Lord's hand. Everything is needed to make up a world. You need creatures of all kinds to make up a creation. You need parishioners of all kinds to make up a parish. You need Christians of all kinds to make up a Christendom.

JEANNETTE

There have been saints of all kinds. There had to be men and women saints of all kinds. And today, we ought to have some. We ought perhaps to have some of yet another kind.

HAUVIETTE

You are among us, you are not like us, you will never be like us. Now me, when I say my prayers, I am glad all the time it lasts. All the time I am saying them and all the time after that. Until the following time. Until the next one.

JEANNETTE

Alas.

HAUVIETTE

But you, it always leaves you hungry to say your prayers. And you are always as unhappy as before. As much after as before. Listen, Jeannette. I know why you want to see Madame Gervaise.

JEANNETTE

No one has guessed it yet, neither mamma, nor my big sister, nor our friend Mengette.

HAUVIETTE

But I know why you want to see her, that Madame Gervaise.

JEANNETTE

Then, Hauviette, that means that you are very unhappy.

HAUVIETTE

Unhappy, unhappy, I am unhappy when it's my turn. It isn't always my turn. But I am a clear-sighted girl. You want to see Madame Gervaise because of the distress of your soul, the distress at the bottom of your soul, at the very bottom of your soul. Here, in the parish, they think that you are happy with this life you lead because you give alms, because you look after the sick and comfort the afflicted and because you are always with those that are sad. But I, Hauviette, know that you are unhappy.

JEANNETTE

You know it because you are my friend, Hauviette.

HAUVIETTE

I am not only your friend, I am a clear-sighted girl. To do good to others, that would do us good, to us girls, if only we did. But you, nothing does you any good. Everything does you harm. Everything leaves you hungry. You are worn away, you are worn away, you are eaten up with sadness, you are pining away with sadness. You are in a fever, poor big sister, a fever of sadness, and you are not getting well, you never get well. You are in a high fever. You are steeped in sadness. Your soul is steeped in sadness. Your uncle went to fetch her, did he.

JEANNETTE

It is true that my soul is sad. Only a while ago . . .

HAUVIETTE

Then why pretend, why do you try to be like other people.

JEANNETTE

Because I am afraid.

HAUVIETTE

Sadness, fear, distress. A big family and there are plenty of them. It is as if you had consumed all the sadness on earth.

JEANNETTE

How should a soul not be steeped in sadness. Only a while ago I saw two little children go by, two urchins, two little fellows walking all alone down yon-

21

der. Behind the birches, behind the hedge. The bigger one dragged the other. They were weeping and screaming: I'm hungry, I'm hungry, I'm hungry . . . I heard them from here. I called to them. I didn't want to leave my sheep. They hadn't seen me. They ran up crying like puppies. The elder one was probably seven.

HAUVIETTE

The smaller one was probably three. Brats, urchins. I know your nurslings very well.

JEANNETTE

Hauviette, Hauviette.

HAUVIETTE

I met them on my way here. I was coming up, they were coming down. They are always coming down. They called me Lady. It was funny. Yes, they said *(she mimics them):* How do you do, Lady. It was awfully funny. They also said: Lady, there is a lady shepherdess minding her sheep up there at the end of the path and spinning wool. Yes indeed, you are the lady shepherdess. *(Slyly.)* They looked well, your two brats did. They looked very well. They were glad. They seemed happy to be alive.

JEANNETTE

They came running like puppies. They screamed: Lady, I'm hungry. Lady, I'm hungry.

HAUVIETTE

You are forgetting something. They must have called you, yes indeed, they certainly called you *(bowing)* Lady shepherdess. They were too keen on doing

22

that. They were too pleased with you, afterwards. And they were too pleased with that, addressing you like that. Not like me.

JEANNETTE

You're not keen on it, you. You are right, you little fool, you little pest. They called me Lady shepherdess.

HAUVIETTE

You see. Me, I don't even notice it. I heard nothing.

JEANNETTE

They cried out: Lady, I'm hungry, Lady, I'm hungry. It went right into my bowels and into my heart, it crushed me as if cries could crush the heart. It hurt me. *(Suddenly looking Hauviette in the eye.)* Perhaps I'm not the only lady who can't stand children's screams.

HAUVIETTE

Come now, shut up. Shut up, I tell you. Who is it you mean? Who is it you're talking about? I don't know her. I don't know any such person. I haven't heard anyone mention her. No, I tell you, I don't know anyone. Wind up your story and let's be done with it. I know your story. Your story bores me stiff. It's no use finishing it. I know how your story ends. You gave them all your bread.

JEANNETTE

I gave them all my bread, my midday meal and my four o'clock meal. They pounced on it like animals; and their joy hurt me and hurts me still, because all of a sudden in spite of myself I caught on, something inside my head began to worry me, all of a sudden, inside my head all was as clear as day; and in spite of myself I thought, I understood, I saw, I thought of all the other starvelings who don't eat, of so many starvelings, innumerable starvelings. I thought of all the poor wretches who are not comforted, of so many and so many poor wretches; I thought of the worst ones of all, of the last, of the very last, of the worst, of those who don't want to be comforted, of so many and so many who don't want to be comforted, who are fed up with comforting and who despair of God's goodness. The poor wretches who grow weary of misfortune and at the same time of consolation itself; they are sooner weary of being comforted than we are of comforting them; as if there were a hollow place in the heart of consolation; as if worms were at it; and when we are still ready to give, they are no longer ready to receive, they no longer wish to receive; they are no longer willing; they no longer hunger to receive; they no longer want to receive anything; how is one to give to him who no longer wants to receive; you would have to have saints; you would have to have new saints who would invent new kinds of consolation. And I felt I was about to cry. So my eyes were swollen, I turned my head because I didn't want them to feel badly, those two, at least.

HAUVIETTE

Yes, yes, you all have invented that too. All that is highly perfected. You have a secret for that. You succeed in suffering more than those who themselves are suffering. Where the poor wretches are unhappy once, you make yourself unhappy one hundred times for the same misfortune. When the poor wretches are unhappy, you are unhappy. When the poor wretches are happy, you are unhappy; for a change. When the poor wretches are unhappy, you are unhappy with them; when the poor wretches are happy, in order to get even, you are still more unhappy. That will have to change, my girl, that will have to change. Or it will end badly. Those two brats were happy while they ate your bread. It meant at least a quarter of an hour's happiness for them. So you all take advantage of that to get an extra quarter of an hour's misery out of it. It is always that much to the good. You are smart. You waste nothing, you take advantage of everything. One more bad quarter of an hour. You know how to turn things to account, you turn everything to account. A quarter of an hour of the worst. It is that much good. It is that much you have earned. You are profiteers.

JEANNETTE

I gave them my bread: much good will it do them! They will be hungry this evening; they will be hungry tomorrow.

HAUVIETTE

They will be hungry this evening, they weren't thinking of it this morning; they were hungry yesterday, they weren't thinking of it this morning. But you thought of it. You are hungry in the place of others. They will find others like you.

You are hungry in the place of others who are hungry, even when they aren't hungry.

JEANNETTE

Fasting, fasting would be nothing. One could fast all the time if it were of any use all the time.

One would fast all the time if it were of any use once. One would fast always if it were of any use.

HAUVIETTE

Neither the worries of tomorrow, nor the worries of yesterday: today only today's worries. We must take what happens as it comes, even what happens to others. We must take what happens as the good Lord sends it, even as he sends it to others, as he sends us what happens to others.

JEANNETTE

Their father was killed by the Burgundians. Alas, alas, it wasn't even the English. To massacre the French. Their mother, alas, their mother. They escaped, both of them, they don't know how. They will never know. The elder one told me about it all, when he was through eating. Before leaving.

(A short pause.)

Here they are once more on the road that makes one hunger. In the dust, in the mud, in hunger. In the future, in distress, in the anxiety about the future. Who will give them, Lord, who will give them their daily bread. But they will, on the contrary, walk in daily distress and hunger. They were still crying as they laughed. And they laughed as they cried, like a ray of sun right through their tears. Their large, forgotten tears rolled and fell on their bread. It was like the last drops of rain when the sun comes back. They ate their bread with what was left of their tears spread on it. What avail our efforts of a day? What avail our charities? I really can't give all the time. I can't give all. I can't give to everyone. I really can't give the passers-by all my father's bread. And even if I did, would it make any difference? Among the mass of the famished. *(She stops spinning by imperceptible degrees.)* For every wounded man we happen to look after, for every child we feed, indefatigable war makes hundreds of wounded, of sick and homeless people, every day. All our efforts are vain. War has more power than anything when it comes to making people suffer. Ah, a curse on war! And a curse on those who brought it to the land of France.

(She has completely stopped spinning. A pause.)

Try as we may, try as we may, they will always go faster than we, they will always do more than we, a deal more than we. All that is needed to set a farm ablaze is a flint. It takes, it took two years to build it. It isn't difficult. One doesn't have to be so clever. It takes months and months, it took work and more work to make the crop grow. And all that is needed to set a crop ablaze is a flint. It takes years and years to make a man grow, it took bread and more bread to feed him, and work and more work, and all kinds of work. And all that is needed to kill him is one blow. One sword thrust and it's done. To make a good Christian, the plough has to work twenty years. To kill a good Christian, the sword has to work one minute. It's always that way. It's like the plough to work twenty years and it's like the sword to work one minute. It's always that way. It's like the plough to work twenty years and it's like the sword to work one minute, and to do more, to be stronger, to make an end of things. So we people will always be the weaker ones. We will always go more slowly, we will always

27

do less. We are the party of those who build up. They are the party of those who pull down. We are the party of the plough. They are the party of the sword. We will always be beaten. They will always get the better of us, on top of us.

No matter what we say.

(A pause.)

For one wounded man dragging himself along the roads, for one man we pick up on the roads, for one child dragging himself along the roadsides, how many people are wounded, and sick, and forsaken, how many women are made unhappy and children forsaken because of the war, and how many are killed, and how many unfortunates lose their souls. Those who kill lose their souls because they kill. And those who are killed lose their souls because they are killed. Those who are strongest, those who kill lose their souls through the murder which they commit. And those who are killed, the man who is weaker, lose their souls through the murder which they suffer, for, seeing how weak they are and how bruised, always the same being weak, and the same unhappy, and the same beaten, and the same killed, then, unhappy ones, they despair of their salvation, because they despair of the goodness of God. Thus, no matter where one may turn, on both sides, it is a game in which, no matter how one plays or what one plays for, salvation is always bound to lose and perdition always bound to win. There is nothing but ingratitude, nothing but despair and perdition.

(A pause.)

And bread everlasting. He who is too much in lack

of daily bread no longer has any desire for bread everlasting, the bread of Jesus Christ.

(A pause.)

Cursed be war, cursed of God; himself; and cursed be those who brought it to the soil of France; and those who brought it to the soil of France, will they have to be cursed, Lord, will they have to be cursed by you. Will we have to ask you for curses, curses against them. And your reprobation. Your business, Lord, is to bless. When we ask for your blessings, we are making you do your job. You were made to shower your blessings like rain, like a beneficent rain, like a soft, lukewarm, pleasant rain, like a fertilizing rain on the earth, like a good rain, like an autumn rain falling on the head, on the heads of your children, all together. Shall it be said, Lord, shall it be said that now we shall ask of you, that we shall have to ask of you curses, your curses, we, all of your children, the ones against the others.

When we ask for your curses, when we ask for your reprobation, we are not making you carry on your business, we are making you do the opposite of your job.

(A pause.)

Lord, Lord, we are not making you do your job.

(A pause. She starts spinning.)

Besides, what does she care about my curses? I could spend my life cursing her, from morning till night, and cities will none the less be forced, and men at arms will none the less ride their horses through time-honored wheat fields.

Sacred, sacred wheat, wheat that make the bread, the flower of the wheat, ear, grain within the ear of wheat. Wheat harvest in the fields. Bread that were served at Our Lord's table. Wheat, bread that were eaten by Our Lord himself, that, one day of days, were eaten.

Wheat, sacred wheat that became the body of Jesus Christ, one day of days, and that are eaten every day, no longer being yourself but the body of Jesus Christ.

(A pause.)

Wheat that are no longer but the aspect of wheat; bread that are no longer but the appearance of bread; bread that are no longer but the species of bread. Bread that are no longer but ancient bread.

(A long pause.)

And you vine, sister of wheat. Grape of the vine cluster. Grapes of the vine-arbor. Vintaging of wine in the vineyards. Vinestalk and grapes of vineyards. Vineyards on the hillsides.

Wine that were served at Our Lord's table. Vine, wine that were drunk by Our Lord himself, that were drunk, one day of days.

Vine, sacred vine, wine that were changed into the blood of Jesus Christ, one day of days, and that are changed every day in the priest's hands, no longer being yourself, but being the blood of Jesus Christ.

(A pause.)

Wine that are no longer but the aspect of wine, wine that are no longer but the appearance of wine; wine that are no longer but the species of wine.

Bread that were changed into the body, wine that were changed into the blood.

Bread that are no longer but ancient bread, wine that are no longer but ancient wine.

(A pause.)

Will it have to be, Lord, that the blood of your Son flowed in vain; that it flowed in vain once, and so many times.

One time, that time; and so many times since.

Will it have to be, Lord, that the body of your Son was offered up in vain; that it was offered up in vain one time, and so many times.

One time, that time, and so many times since.

Will it be said that you will forsake, that you have forsaken your children's Christendom.

All is full of war and perdition. And war it is that makes perdition. Will it be said that you have given us up to war.

(A pause.)

It is you we need and the sight of your hand passing over the earth.

You did it in days gone by. You did it for other peoples. Won't you do it for this people of France.

For other peoples you have sent saints. You have even sent warriors.

We are sinners, but we are Christians just the same. We are Christian people. We belong to your people of Christendom.

(A pause.)

Otherwise, what does she care about our curses. We could spend our whole life cursing her, from morning till night as one says his prayers. She was cursed by Jesus and the trollop is none the worse for it, it's appalling. She has had upon her the curse, the reprobation of Jesus himself, Saint Peter and the sword of Malchus, Malchus and Saint Peter's sword. With what power and by what authority are we then going to curse her. It is appalling that there should be someone with the curse of Jesus upon her and walking about as a conqueror on all the highways of the world. Will you then deliver up the world to that trollop?

(A pause.)

But with what power can we little ones curse her, and with what efficiency. I would have done much better to quietly go on spinning. As long as there isn't someone who will kill the trollop, who will murder murder and save this people, as long as there isn't someone who will kill war, we shall be like children when they play down below in the fields at building dams and levees with earth and sand, with mud out of the Meuse River. The Meuse always ends by submerging it.

One day or other.

HAUVIETTE

And is that why you want to see Madame Gervaise?

JEANNETTE

. . .

HAUVIETTE

Madame Gervaise, who isn't your friend . . .

JEANNETTE

You can't be friends with a saint.

HAUVIETTE

(With great violence.)

She is less of a saint than you are.

JEANNETTE

(Receiving the blow with a blush and closing her eyes for a moment.)

Be quiet, wretched girl, how dare you say such a thing? She is a holy woman.

HAUVIETTE

I am a clear-sighted girl. You can't be friends with a holy woman.

JEANNETTE

Madame Gervaise is in a convent. No maid enters a convent unless God calls her by her name. There is a vocation. There must be a vocation. No maid enters a convent, no soul takes refuge in a convent, no soul, with its body, alas, unless God has summoned it, by its name, has instructed, ordered, designated it by its name, led it by the hand, and sometimes compelled it and taken it for himself. There must be a vocation. God must have fixed its destiny. Named it. So God has no doubt revealed unto them, God must have told them things that we don't know, some things of which we people are ignorant. God must have granted them private revelations.

HAUVIETTE

There is no such thing as private revelations. There is only one revelation for everybody, and that's the revelation of God and of Our Lord Jesus Christ. Of

God by himself and by Our Lord Jesus Christ. It is a revelation for all good Christians, for all Christians, even for the bad ones, and for sinners, for all good parishioners. For every man and every woman, for each person in the parish. Be it known to all persons in the parish. That there is a promise of salvation . . . Between God and his creature. Be it known. When the trumpet calls and the drum rolls before a proclamation at wheat harvesting, the proclamation is made for everyone, for all the harvesters. And after the harvest, when a proclamation is made for gleaning, it is made for everyone, the proclamation for gleaning, for all the gleaners, for all the poor women who go out to glean, to pick up ears of wheat in the fields, ears of wheat that have been dropped from the sheaves. When the proclamation for vintaging is made, it is made for all, for all the vintagers. And after vintaging, when the proclamation for gleaning in vineyards is made, it is made for all the poor good women who go and glean, for all the old good women who go and pick up what is left on the vinestalks, and what was not quite ripe at the time of vintaging. Everything that was still a little green, a little greenish. Now for fourteen centuries they have been making a proclamation of salvation. For all the parishes. For all persons in all parishes. It is the common revelation. The Christian revelation. The parochial revelation. The good Lord has called everyone, he has summoned everyone, he has named everyone. His Providence provides. His Providence foresees. His Providence watches over everyone, sees everyone, sees for everyone. His sight extends over everyone. He leads everyone by the hand. He has designated all of us women. We have all of us entered the convent of Christendom. We have all taken refuge in the great convent of Christendom. God has instructed all of us, called all of us, commanded all of us. We all belong to the house, to the same house, and it is God who leads the whole household. He has called us all by our names, which are our Christian names. To all of us he has made the same revelation, which is that we shall all go to heaven if we live like good Christians. He sent us all the same vocation, to go to heaven when our turn comes if we live like good Christians. There is no one that comes closer to God than the others. Every word from man or woman, from father, mother or children comes straight to God's ear. Every word from the lips, every word from the heart. And you all, the big ones, you who have begun, you all who have made your first communion, you see, you eat the good Lord directly, you are given God directly as nourishment.

(Jeanne bends her head.)

And you can't come closer than by touching. There is nothing closer than food. Than taking food into one's body, than the incarnation of food.

Prayer is the same for all. Sacraments are the same for all.

We too have been called by baptism, by our baptism, to be good Christian girls, to be Christian girls. And we have been called to be good girls, and to please our fathers and mothers, and to look after our little brothers and sisters, and all that must be done the whole blessed day.

JEANNETTE

Madame Gervaise is in the convent: the holy founders, men and women. There have been so many great saints, and such great saints, at the founding of convents, that all their holiness must be transferred, must be poured back particularly upon those who are called to their convents.

HAUVIETTE

Our Lord Jesus Christ is the first among saints and the first among founders. He is the greatest saint and the greatest founder. And all his holiness is transferred, is poured back upon all those who bear the name of Christian.

On all who are called Christian.

All his merit, all his holiness is eternally poured back.

JEANNETTE

The merits, the great merits of holy founders and foundresses must act more particularly in favor of the daughters and sons whom vocation has given them.

HAUVIETTE

The merits of Our Lord Jesus Christ, which are the greatest merits, which are merits without end, work together for the benefit of all Christendom.

For all of us, for us who are his daughters and sons.

Who are his brothers and sisters.

All his daughters and all his sons, all his brothers and all his sisters that baptism has given him.

That the vocation of baptism has given him.

There is the communion of saints; and it begins

with Jesus. He is in it. He is at the head. All prayers, all trials together, all works, all merits, all the virtues of Jesus together and all the virtues of the other saints together, all sainthoods together work and pray for the whole world together, for the whole of Christendom, for the salvation of the whole world. Together.

I am a clear-sighted little French girl; and I don't let people bamboozle me. I am a clear-sighted little girl from Lorraine.

JEANNETTE

Madame Gervaise is in a convent. She must know why the good Lord allows so much suffering to exist. So much suffering and so much perdition.

HAUVIETTE

Do you know exactly how Gervaise went into a convent?

JEANNETTE

Yes: Madame Colette, who is a saint, came by here. She converted Gervaise with three of her friends.

HAUVIETTE

Her mother cried a good deal at that time.

Jeannette, Jeannette, suppose we all did the same.

Our Lord Jesus Christ did not go into a monastery. He did not live in a monastery. He lived with his father and mother, like a bachelor. He was a carpenter; by profession. And after that, he didn't retire. On the contrary, for three years he went and preached publicly.

JEANNETTE

I wanted to see Madame Colette, but she has a

37

great many souls to save. So I told my uncle to go and find Madame Gervaise at Nancy.

To go and fetch Madame Gervaise.

HAUVIETTE

Since she entered a convent her mother is alone and is bored and weeps and what a sad sight it is.

JEANNETTE

She came at once, I am expecting her this morning.

HAUVIETTE

The last time there were soldiers, her mother fled to the island with us; but there wasn't anyone with her to take away her belongings; *I* couldn't help her to carry her belongings, because mamma needed me. My poor Jeannette, my poor Jeannette, she fled then like a poor old woman all alone. It was awful, it was awful. It made one cry. It broke one's heart, it was pitiful. But there was nothing to be done about it. She bent her back as she ran. I see her still. It was disgraceful. One felt like lending her some children. So then, after that, when she came back to her home, when she walked back into her house, she found nothing at all of what she had before: the soldiers had stolen everything. One felt ashamed for her.

She fled like a poor old grandmother of a woman with no children.

(A brief pause.)

Truly Madame Gervaise had badly chosen her time to leave the world and save her soul.

(A pause.)

Listen, Jeannette. One must not do like her and fly

38

to a convent to save one's own soul. One must not
save one's soul as one saves a treasure.

JEANNETTE

Alas, alas, it is nonetheless the greatest treasure.
It is the only treasure.

HAUVIETTE

Then it must be saved as one loses a treasure. In
spending it. We must save ourselves together in spending it. We must arrive together at the good Lord's.
We must not go looking for the good Lord the ones
without the others. We must all go back together to
our father's house. We must also think a little of
others. We must work a little for others. What would
he say to us if we arrived, if we came back the ones
without the others.

JEANNETTE

So then you insist on it? On our making dams together and earth-banks, with the earth and mud from
the river, with the sand, before this river of perdition?

HAUVIETTE

Come now, Jeannette, don't lose your temper. You
are right. The best thing would be, if it were possible,
to kill war, as you say.

JEANNETTE

The match is uneven. There had to be Jesus to
bring about salvation, Jesus and all the saints.

HAUVIETTE

The other saints.

JEANNETTE

Twenty centuries, I know not how many centuries of prophets. Fourteen centuries of Christendom. Only one moment is needed to damn a soul. Only one moment is needed for perdition.

It's always the same thing, the match is not even. War wages war on peace. And peace, of course, does not wage war on war. Peace leaves war in peace. Peace kills itself through war. And war does not kill itself through peace. Since it did not kill itself through God's peace, through the peace of Jesus Christ, how should it kill itself through man's peace?

Through a man's peace.

HAUVIETTE

You are right, big sister, you are right. The best thing, if one could, would be to kill war, as you say. But in order to kill war, you have to make war; in order to kill war, you need a war lord, *(laughing as she would at the most enormous joke, at the most unthinkable flight of fancy;)* and it isn't us, is it, who are going to make war? It isn't us who will ever be war lords? So while we wait until they have killed war, we've got to work, each in his place, each doing his best, keeping safe everything that hasn't yet been spoiled.

Each in our place.

JEANNETTE

Those soldiers, those soldiers who are of no use except for perdition. Still, in the old days, there were people who were useful for everything. Sometimes for salvation and sometimes for perdition. But now they

37244

work only for perdition. In the old days, there were professions, each had his profession; and in their professions, they sometimes worked for perdition, but sometimes they worked for salvation. And now it's perdition all the time. Those men have made it their profession. How can one imagine such misery, such a sorry sight. Lord, Lord, how can you, why do you allow it? Men who have a profession; and that profession is always to destroy, to procure, to bring about the perdition of souls.

HAUVIETTE

Jeannette, listen to me well.

For well nigh fifty years and more, according to the old folks, the soldier has been harvesting as he chooses; for well nigh fifty years and more, the soldier has been crushing, or burning, or robbing the ripe harvest as he chooses; the least he does is to tread the ripe harvest under his horse's hoofs. Now then, after all that time, each year, in the fall, the good ploughman, your father, my father, your two big brothers, our friends' fathers, always the same, the same peasants, the same French peasants, plough the same fields with just the same care, before God, the fields yonder, when they sow their seed. That is what preserves everything. Destroyed houses are rebuilt. Churches, even churches, destroyed parishes are rebuilt. The parish has never ceased to work. And with all these entanglements, worship, divine worship has never ceased. That is what keeps everything. They are good Christians. Mass has never ceased; nor vespers; nor any service, nor any of God's services. And they never failed to do their Easter duty, at least once a year. That is what

41

keeps everything. Work. The good Lord's work. All they would have to do, would be to become soldiers too; it isn't difficult: you receive fewer blows, because you hand some out to others. Once they were soldiers, they would just have to harvest without having sowed. But good ploughmen like good fields to plough and good sowings. . . .

(As if correcting herself.)

Listen, I wouldn't want to speak foolishly. But at least I believe that they like ploughing and sowing just as much as harvesting. At least they like ploughing as much as harvesting and sowing as much as reaping, because all of that is work, the same work, the same blessed work before God.

After all they don't want to harvest without having ploughed, to reap without having sowed. It wouldn't be fair. It wouldn't be according to the good Lord's order.

Every year in the same season they do the same job with the same courage, the whole year long the same work with the same patience: that is what holds everything together, what keeps everything; they are the ones who hold everything together, who keep everything, who save all that can be saved; it is thanks to them that all is not yet dead, and the good Lord will surely end by blessing their crops.

I am like them. If I were at home busy spinning my weight of wool, or which amounts to the same, if I were playing lumberman, because it was playtime; and if someone came and told me, if someone came running: Hauviette, Hauviette! It is the hour of judgment, the hour of last judgment, in half an hour the angel is going to begin blowing his trump . . .

JEANNETTE

Wretched, wretched girl, how dare you talk of such a thing?

HAUVIETTE

I would go on spinning my wool and it comes to the same I would go on playing lumberman.

JEANNETTE

Hauviette, Hauviette . . .

HAUVIETTE

Because the play of creatures is agreeable to God. Little girls' fun, little girls' innocence is agreeable to God. Children's innocence is God's greatest glory. Everything one does in the day is agreeable to God, provided of course that it is all right. Everything is God's, everything concerns God, everything is done before God's eyes; the whole day is God's. All prayer is God's, all work is God's; all play too is God's, when it's time to play. I am a little French girl, I am not afraid of God because he is our father. My father does not frighten me. The morning prayer and the evening prayer, the morning *Angelus* and the evening *Angelus,* the three meals a day and *goûter* at four o'clock and appetite for meals and grace before meals, work between meals and play when it's time for it and amusement when it's possible, prayers when rising because the day is beginning, prayers when retiring because the day is ending and the night is beginning, asking first, thanking after, always being in a good temper, it is for all these things taken together and for all these things one after the other that we have been put on earth, it is all these things together, all these things one after the other that make up God's

43

day. If in a little while I were told: You know, Hauviette, it is going to happen in half an hour . . .

JEANNETTE
My little Hauviette, my little Hauviette.

HAUVIETTE
I would go on spinning, if I happened to be spinning, and playing, if I happened to be playing. And on arriving, I'd say to the good Lord: Our Father, who art in heaven, I am little Hauviette, of the parish of Domremy in Lorraine; at your service; of your parish of Domremy in your Lorraine of Christendom. You called us back somewhat early, seeing that I was still a very small girl. But you are a good father and you know what you are doing.

(A pause.)

I am an obstinate little French girl. Never can you make me believe that one must be afraid of the good Lord; that one can be afraid of the good Lord. When I am on the road and my father calls me to make me go back home, I am not afraid of my father.

(A pause.)

I am like them. We are their daughters. Less strength is needed to knock down a man than to fell a tree. Less trouble is needed, it is easier to be a soldier than to be a woodman, it is easier to be a soldier than to be a peasant; it is easier, it is more agreeable, so it seems, they say so at least, one would think, it would appear that it is more agreeable to be executioner than victim. It is nevertheless an extraordinary fact, it is one of the greatest proofs, it is one of the

44

greatest tokens of God's goodness that there should be for all that as many peasants as soldiers, as many martyrs as executioners; as many peasants as required, as many martyrs, as many victims as required; always as many of one kind as of the other; it is the greatest proof of God's presence among us, that they can do as they will, that one would think everything was done to make certain professions impossible, to discourage certain professions, and that there are always as many working in those professions, as many as are required to keep the world going. And that one can't discourage peasants, and that one can't discourage victims and martyrs. And that soldiers will grow weary before peasants, and that executioners will grow weary before victims and martyrs.

One believes, one might believe that it is better to be in the place of the executioner than in the place of the victim, in the place of the executioner than in the place of the martyr. It must be that there is a mistake.

JEANNETTE

It has now been over fifty years, Hauviette, that the good ploughmen have been praying the good Lord for the welfare of the crops; it has now been over eight years that little me has been praying with all her might for the welfare of the crops. Madame Gervaise is at the convent; she should know why the good Lord does not answer good prayers.

HAUVIETTE

I am a good Christian. I am a good French girl. If we want the good Lord to bless the crops, Jeannette, we must first sow the seed; that is why we begin by doing that each year. Then when the well-prepared soil is well sowed, we say our prayers that the soldier may not come, that the new wheat may come up and grow into a crop. That the crop may increase and the wheat be plentiful. As for us, it is all we can do, it is all we have to do; the rest concerns the good Lord; we are in his hand; he is the master; he grants our wishes according to his will.

JEANNETTE

God grants fewer and fewer of our wishes, Hauviette. The travelers that pass this way no longer bring any but bad news. The English have encompassed the mount of Lord Saint Michael, and now the wheat which was lacking to make bread will be lacking as well for the sowing.

HAUVIETTE

It is the good Lord's business: our wheat is his. When I have done my work properly and said my prayers properly, he grants my wishes according to his will; it isn't for us, nor for anyone to ask him what his reasons are. Really, Jeannette, you must be in very great pain to dare to call the good Lord to account in this way. To ask him what his reasons are. To try to pick a quarrel with him.

You yourself work properly. You work like everyone else. You work better than I do. You work better than anyone. You spin wool; wool, the one thing useful. You work more than I do. This morning you will have worked more than I. I talk and at the same time do nothing. You talk and at the same time you work.

46

Restless girl, insatiable soul, restless soul, if you believe what you say, then at least don't work.

JEANNETTE

It is true: I am in great pain because of all that perdition; but I have another pain to bear, an unknown pain, beyond all that you could imagine.

HAUVIETTE

You will probably tell Madame Gervaise about it, about this new pain of yours.

JEANNETTE

I don't know.

(A pause.)

HAUVIETTE

Goodbye, my pretty one, see you later. *(Pointing to the path leading to the market town.)* She will come this way. *(Pointing to the path going right, along the hillside.)* As for me, I am going this way. I have something to attend to there. I don't know how it happens. I always have something to attend to elsewhere. I don't know. I never met her, never met that person. I have always had something to attend to elsewhere. Where she doesn't happen to be. There are coincidences of that kind in life. It surprises me, too, that I have never met her.

This way. That way.

It is disgraceful. It is terrible. Now her mother bears the good Lord a grudge. Her mother is jealous of the good Lord. Her mother reproaches the good Lord. She reproaches the good Lord with having stolen her daughter. It is godlessness, godlessness such

47

as had never been seen. Unspeakable. Her mother said that thing, that the good Lord was a thief.

That he had stolen her daughter.

Unspeakable godlessness.

What did it all lead to.

I'd rather think of your two nurselings. Perhaps the good Lord will send that they find people like you, tomorrow. In spite of which you are right. People like you, if there are any, are few in number. If there are any, there are not many.

Goodbye. Eat your meals heartily. Say your prayers heartily.

(Exit.)

JEANNETTE
(A long pause.)

Lord, Lord, what is the matter? At all times, alas, at all times people have lost their souls; but for the last forty years alas they have done nothing but that, they have done nothing but lose their souls. What is the matter, Lord, what is the matter. There were still some who saved their souls. There were some who came through. But now, Lord, who could be sure that some are saved, who could be sure that just a few, even just a few, even the smallest possible number, come through. It used to be in the world, alas, sometimes, often it was the world that made one ready for hell. Nowadays even that is no longer true; it is no longer the world that makes one ready for hell. It is hell itself overflowing on earth. What is the matter, Lord, what is it that has changed, what is there that's new. What have you done with this people, with your Christian people. Must it be that you

48

have sent your son in vain and will it be said that Jesus died in vain, your son who died for us. Will it be said that you have not put a stop to this great sorrow in the kingdom of France.

(A pause.)

Jesus, Jesus, one day on a mountain in that country you felt sorry for the people, you wept over that crowd, and that crowd was hungry and in order to feed it, to stay its body's hunger, to sate its bodily hunger you multiplied the fishes and loaves.

Jesus, Jesus, Jesus, today your people is hungry and you do not sate your people. Today in this country your people of today, in your Lorraine of Christendom, in your France of Christendom, in your Christendom your people of Christendom are hungry. They lack everything. They lack bodily bread. They lack spiritual bread. And in order to nourish them, to sate their one and other hunger, to give them the body's bread and the soul's bread will it be said that you are no longer among us. Will it be said that you no longer multiply, that you will not multiply the dried fishes and the loaves.

You will not weep over this multitude.

(A pause. In a vision.)

Blessed are those who saw him pass by in his country; blessed are those who saw him walk on this earth; who saw him walk on the temporal lake; blessed are those who saw him raise Lazarus. When one thinks, Lord, when one thinks that it happened only once. When one thinks, Lord, when one thinks. When one thinks that he was a man like all the others, an ordinary man; apparently like all the others, apparently ordinary. He walked on the road like an ordinary man; his feet rested on the ground; and he walked up the paths on the hillside. Jerusalem, Jerusalem, you were more blessed than Rome. Truly, truly, you were more favored, Jerusalem, you were more fortunate. A man like the others. And you, Nazareth, little market town, little town of Judea, you were happier than Reims and Saint-Denis. And you, Bethlehem, little market town of Judea, the smallest of market towns of Judea, the most brilliant of the market towns of Judea, you will also shine eternally above all the market towns of the earth, you will shine eternally above all the market towns of Christendom, eternally and infinitely above our obscure market towns, our little Christian parishes. Who will ever know this little parish of Domremy. Who will ever even know the name of this little parish of Domremy. Who will even know that it ever existed.

And thou Bethlehem in the land of Judea, art not the least among the princes of Judea: for out of thee shall come forth a Governor, that shall rule my people Israel.

But you, Christian parishes, parishes of Lorraine, French parishes, you have been less favored. The greatest among you, the holiest among you, those among you that are fullest, that are most crammed with holiness, the greatest in holiness among you all have nothing that can approach, even from the furthest possible point, what was given that little out-of-the-way market town. You Chartres, a city unique in France, cathedral unique in the world, Chartres, diocese, city unique in the kingdom of France, Chartres

50

who are consecrated, dedicated, given to Our Lady, Chartres who are vowed, what are you, Chartres, great city, in comparison with this little market town. And you too are nothing, Saint-Michel, unique market town, city unique in the world, unique in all Christendom, basilica of the world. And you Tours, city of the Loire, city of Saint Martin, you who were capital of the Gauls, who in this country, in the kingdom of France were capital of the first Christian communities. Metropolis, mother city, mother of the other cities. All of you, what are you, great dioceses, great cities, great parishes, what are you by the side of this little market town, compared with this obscure market town, which alas alas, is perhaps no longer even a parish, a Christian parish. And you, towers of Notre-Dame, Paris, who were capital of the kingdom of France, doubly consecrated, doubly dedicated, doubly given, bound by a twofold vow, both to you, Our Lady, and to our great Saint Genevive; what are you. And you too, Orléans, you finally are nothing, Orléans, city of the Loire, dedicated to great Saint Aignan. Great cities, illustrious cities, cities of Christendom, you have great saints and great patrons, the holiest, the greatest patrons in the world, and above all saints you have received patronage, you have the Blessed Virgin Our Lady. You have given both birth and trouble to great saints and they will eternally watch over you, eternally be your patrons, for eternally seated at the right hand they will pray for you. They will eternally protect you, eternally cover you up with their prayers. Now you are nothing, Christian cities, great cities, residences of Christendom, seats, cathedrals of holiness, you are nothing. For everything has been taken, once for all, and nothing remains to be taken. Everything has been taken, everything that counts, once for all, one day forever. And nothing remains, children, there is nothing to be taken of all that counts. For verily I tell you that that little out-of-the-way market town took everything, one day, once in time; once in eternity; once for all, one time for all times; one day, stealthily, it took forever everything that counts. And you, great cities, Christian cities, what is left for you. What are you. For you lag behind producing saints, and during that time, Jesus is the saint of that parish, which alas is perhaps no longer a parish. A Christian one. Or even a parish. Others have Saint Loup and Saint Gratien; others have Saint Francis; others have Our Lady herself. You people of Picardy you have other saints, and other saints too, you people of the country around Bourges. And you Nancy, nearby city, nearby parishes, you all, you people of Nancy, you have great Saint Nicholas. You Toul, our diocese, you have what you have. *(Turning a little more toward the church.)* And you my parish you have great Saint Remi. But where are you headed, parishes. During that time Jesus himself is the very saint, the saint, the patron of that parish. While you are lagging behind. You lag behind producing saints, ordinary saints, Lord, and during that time, while no one suspected it, without warning anyone in this country, while no one was on his guard, without our fathers and grandfathers having received the least warning, in this country, and yet they were such good people, a little market town came along, having already taken everything. To that parish was given what never was given to you, parishes of France, what never in all eternity will be given to any other parish. To any parish. When no one expected it. For it was accomplished, it was accomplished once for all, one day in time, in that country, one time for all times, in eternity once for ever, in all eternity for all eternity. And he came by night like a thief. And never again will it be done. You are lagging behind, parishes, you are lagging behind, bringing forth the greatest saints. And during that time, without any warning, without telling anyone, a little no-account parish had given birth to the holy of holies. In a flash of lightning it succeeded, it had done what will never be done again, it had made, given birth to the one who will never again be born. And just as you, parishes, have Saint Crépin and Saint Crépinien for patrons, so you, Bethlehem, have Saint Jesus for patron. Others have Saint Marceau and Saint Donatien: and Rome has Saint Peter. But you, Bethlehem, obscure little parish, little out-of-the-way parish, you clever one have Saint Jesus, and no one will ever be able to take him away from you, in all eternity. For he is your patron, as Saint Ouen is the patron of Rouen. For it is that saint you have given birth to; one day of the world you brought him into the world. You brought forth that saint, you gave birth to that saint. And we people are nothing but little people.

And there will be no other kind of people but little people, since a parish came along and took all to itself.

Even before anyone else had begun.

There will never again, in all eternity, be other people than little people.

(A pause.)

Happy is she who poured on his feet the ointment of the amphora, she who poured on his head the ointment of the alabaster box, at Bethany, in the house of Simon who was called the leper; on his feet, on his very feet, on his body of flesh, on his very head, on the head of his body; happy are they all, men and women, happy all in a heap, sinners and saints. To the sinners of that time, Lord, to the sinners of that time and of that country was granted what you withheld, O Lord, from saints, what you did not grant your saints of all times. To the greatest sinners of that time and of that place was granted what was not given to the greatest saints of the greatest centuries. What has not been given since. Ever. To anyone. Happy is she who with a handkerchief, a real handkerchief, a handkerchief to blow one's nose in, an imperishable handkerchief wiped that majestic face, his very face, his real face, his man's face with a white handkerchief that perishable face; his pitiful face; and to see him then, in that state, the saviour of the human race, to see him thus, him, the saviour of all the human race, what unfeeling heart would not have softened, what eyes, what human eyes would not have shed tears; that face in a perspiration, all covered with sweat, and filth, and dust, all covered with the dust of the roads, all covered with the dust of the soil; the dust of his face, the common dust, everybody's dust, the dust on his face; stuck to it with sweat. Happy Magdalen, happy Veronica; happy Saint Magdalen, happy Saint Veronica, you are not saints like the other ones. All the saints among men are saints, all the saints among

54

women are saints, but you are not saints like the others. All saints, men and women, are seated with Jesus at the right of the Father. All saints, men and women, contemplate Jesus seated at the right of the Father. And there he has, in heaven he has his man's body, his human body in a state of glory, since he went up to heaven, as he was, on Ascension Day. But you, you alone, you saw, you touched, you grasped that human body in its humanity, in your common humanity, walking and seated on our common earth. You alone have seen him on the ground. You alone have seen him twice and not once only; not one time only, like all the others, in your eternity; not only the second time, which lasts forever; but a first time, a previous time, an earthly time; and that is what was given once only, that is what was not given to all. There are several classes of saints, there are two, and you belong to the first, and we, all of us, sinners and saints, we come behind and are nothing but eleventh-hour laborers; and the saints themselves, the other saints in heaven, are afterwards, from now on they are but saints of the eleventh hour. For they see him only in eternity, when one has time, and you, you see him also in eternity, and you had seen him, you have seen him on earth, when one does not have time. Unique event, earthly event, which went by so quickly, which will not occur again. Awful mystery, you came near that awful mystery. Cathedral towns, you did not see that. You enclose in your cathedrals centuries of prayer, centuries of sacraments, centuries of holiness, the holiness of a whole people, ascending from a whole people, but you did not see that. And they did. All of them saw it, without going out of their way, those who were there and those who had come there, those who had come on purpose and those who had not come on purpose; the shepherds, the magi, and the ass, and the ox that blew on him to keep him warm. He was within call, he was within hand-reach, within reach of eyes, within reach of a look from the eyes, and that will not occur again. Reims, you are the city of the coronation. You are therefore the finest city of the kingdom of France. And there is no finer ceremony in the world, there is not so fine a ceremony in the world as the coronation of the king of France, in any country. But whence come you, city of Reims, what are you doing, cathedral of Reims. Who are you. A stable, in that out-of-the-way market town, a poor stable, in that poor little out-of-the-way market town of Bethlehem, a stable which saw the birth of a reign that will never perish, a simple stable, a reign that will never disappear in centuries of centuries, never, a stable that saw the birth of a king who will reign forever. In that country. That is what they do in that country. And the king of France, who is the greatest king in the world, makes solemn entries, makes a solemn entry in Reims, and nothing is more beautiful than the king's entry in Reims, nothing is more beautiful in the world, nothing in the world is as beautiful, in the whole world; and twenty kings of France, in Reims, in the cathedral of Reims, have made twenty solemn entries, twenty sumptuous entries. But you Jerusalem are more blessed, you are blessed among all cities; you are infinitely greater, and more blessed, and more honored. You have received an honor infinitely greater. You are blessed above the heads of all cities, for he entered within

56

your walls, seated on the colt of an ass; and that will not occur again; and the people of that country threw palms and leaves, boughs and flowers under the ass's feet. Our parishes saw the birth of, gave birth to, brought forth other saints. But those parishes saw the birth of, gave birth to, brought forth the greatest saint, the holy of holies: what a distinction. While you were having fun, Christian parishes, producing saints, a parish rose early in the morning. Rose before anyone else. And brought forth the saint that will never again be created. Blessed is the man that happened to be there, just at the moment when his cross had to be borne, to help him bear his cross, a heavy cross, his real cross, that heavy wooden cross, made of real wood, his cross of torment, a heavy, well-constructed cross. As it was for everyone, for all the others who were tormented in the same torment. A man who was passing that way, no doubt. Ah, well had he chosen his time, had that one, that man who passed that way, just at that point, just then, just at that moment. That man who was passing just there. How many men since, numberless men in centuries of centuries would have wanted to be there, in his place, to go by, to have gone by just at that moment. Just there. But there you are, it was too late, it was he who had gone by, and in eternity, in centuries of centuries, he would not yield his place to others; and they, the late-comers, they were obliged to fall back on other crosses, to exert themselves, to go through exercises, to fall back on bearing other crosses. On making other crosses by themselves. On having some made for them. Artificially. That doesn't come to the same. A man of Cyrene, called Simon, whom they *compelled* to bear the cross of Jesus. He is no longer in need today of being compelled to *have borne* the cross of Jesus. Blessed above all, blessed is that one, and he too would not yield his place to another, not he, blessed is that one who yet saw him but once. Blessed is he, blessed above all, blessed above all men, the most blessed of all, blessed is he who saw him in time, and who yet saw him but once. Blessed is he who saw him in the temple; and after that; because that was enough; was recalled like a good servant. He was an old man of that country; a man who was nearing the close of the day and who touched the close of the day, at the close of the last day of his life. But he did not see his last day setting without having seen the eternal sun rising. Blessed is that man who took the child Jesus in his arms, who held him up with his two hands, the little child Jesus, as one takes, as one holds up an ordinary child, a little child of a family of ordinary men; with his old tanned hands, with his old wrinkled hands, with his poor withered and puckered-up old man's hands, with his two shriveled-up hands. With his two parchment-like hands. *And, behold, there was a man in Jerusalem, whose name was Simeon: and the same was just and devout, waiting for the consolation of Israel: and the Holy Ghost was upon him. And it was revealed unto him by the Holy Ghost, that he should not see death, before he had seen the Lord's Christ.*

And he came by the Spirit into the temple: and when the parents brought in the child Jesus, to do for him after the custom of the law,

Then he took him up in his arms, and blessed God, and said,

58

*Lord, now lettest thou thy servant depart in peace,
according to thy word.*

For mine eyes have seen the salvation,

*Which thou hast prepared before the face of all
people;*

*A light to lighten the Gentiles, and the glory of
thy people Israel.*

*And his father and his mother marveled at those
things which were spoken of him.*

Waiting for the consolation of Israel; and the consolation came; and the consolation was not sufficient.
The consolation came, and the consolation failed to
console.

The consolation failed to console Israel; it also
failed to console your Christendom, Lord.

Waiting for the consolation of Israel; for fifty years,
Lord, for fourteen centuries, for fifty years we have
waited for the consolation of your Christendom.

Waiting for the consolation of Israel; of the kingdom of Israel; how long, Lord, will we be waiting for
the consolation of the kingdom of France; the consolation of the great distress in the kingdom of France.

The consolation came; and it has not consoled
enough; it has not sufficiently consoled.

But he, that old man, that old man from that country, we don't know if he saw anything else after that.
And blessed was he in knowing no more. Blessed, the
most blessed of all, he knew no more of what happened on earth.

That one indeed could also boast that he had been
at the right place. He had held, for he had held, in

his weak hands, the greatest *dauphin* in the world, the
son of the greatest king; a king himself, the son of the
greatest king; a king himself Jesus Christ; in his hands
he had held up the king of kings, the greatest king in
the world, king above kings, above all the kings of
the world.

He had held in his hands the greatest kingdom's
kingship in the world.

And he knew of no other event on earth.

For at the close of his life, at the close of his day,
at one go, at the first go, he had known the greatest
event on earth.

And also the greatest event in heaven.

The greatest event in the world.

The greatest event of any time.

The only great event of any time.

The greatest event in the world.

The only interesting event that ever took place.

And so anyone could come near you. And that old
man, at the close of his life, kissed you like an ordinary little child. Surely he kissed you. Like an old
man, as old people like to kiss children, little ones,
tiny children. But you, spire of Chartres, nave of
Amiens, where are you going. What are you doing,
who are you, where do you come from. You are nothing. And you spire of Chartres and tombs of Saint-
Denis, holy things of the kingdom of France, you are
nothing. And in this little country, in this little market town, in this little parish they have seen what was
not seen at Château-Thierry; in that other little parish of that country, where there may not even be a

church, at present; today; they saw there what was never seen at Château-Thierry. Another parish had risen earlier in the morning. How did they go about it, Lord, the people of that time and of that country, the people of that day and of that place. What did they mean to you, what had they meant to you, the men of that time and of that country. What a mystery, what an awful mystery. What an awe-inspiring mystery. All they had to do was to come near that awe-inspiring mystery. Those who happened to be there just at the right moment. Without doing anything to that effect they had, they have had what had been refused; necessarily; since it could happen just once; naturally it could happen just once. What was not given to the greatest saints of other times and other countries. All they had to do was to come near that awe-inspiring mystery. The last of that time and of that country have had what the first among us, the holiest, the greatest saints among us will never have in all eternity. What a mystery, Lord, what a mystery. When you think, when you think, that's where we should have been, all that was needed was to be born just there, at that time and in that country. Lord, Lord, you have given your tormentors what was refused to so many of your martyrs. The Roman soldier who pierced your side had what so many of your saints, so many of your martyrs did not have. Unto him was it given to touch you. Unto him, to see you. He had one look on earth from your mercy. He had one look on earth from your own eyes. Blessed were those who drank the look from your eyes; blessed were those who ate the bread from your table; and Judas, Judas himself was able to come near you.

Blessed were those who drank the milk of your words. Blessed were those who ate, one day, one unique day, one day among all days, blessed with a unique happiness, blessed were those who ate one day, one unique day, that holy Thursday, blessed were those who ate the bread of your body; you yourself consecrated by yourself; in a unique consecration; one day that will never come again; when you yourself said the first mass; on your own body; when you celebrated the first mass; when you consecrated yourself; when of that bread, before the twelve, and before the twelfth, the thirteenth, you made your body; and when of that wine, you made your blood; that day when you were at once the victim and the priest, the same being the victim and the priest, the offering and the offertory, the bread and the baker, the wine and the cup-bearer; the bread and he who gives the bread; the wine and he who pours out the wine; the flesh and the blood, the bread and the wine. That time when you were the priest and they were the faithful, that time when you were the priest in action, offering up a sacrifice for the first time. That time when you invented the priest, the first priest in action, offering up a sacrifice for the first time. And you were all in one the priest and the victim. That time when you made the first sacrifice. When you were the first one sacrificed, the first Host. The first victim. To think, Lord, to think that you were there, that all that was needed was to come near you, awe-inspiring mystery. Really, to think that it happened once. That it was once seen on earth. That everyone could touch you, *visible shepherd*, the womenfolk, the children, the beggars on the highways. And that you spoke like a simple man who speaks. What indeed did they do to you, Lord, all those people, to be honored with that honor, favored, benefited, blessed, graced with that grace. And you, Jews, Jewish people, people of Jewry, what indeed did that people do to you, that you preferred it to all peoples; that you should have thus made it pass before all peoples. What indeed did they do to you, *what did he do to you that you have chosen him?* That you have thus laden (this people) with this grace; that you have thus preferred it to the others, chosen it among the others above all the others. That you have shed such lustre upon it, everlasting lustre. That from century to century, and I am counting first of all the centuries of the earth, that you have taken from it, among it the line of prophets, the race of prophets. From century to century, step by step, from generation to generation, from ascension to ascension the slow ascension, the line of prophets, the race of prophets. What people, Lord, would not have deemed itself happy, what people among so many peoples, what people among countless peoples, in being your people; what people would not have wished to be in its place; a chosen people; a chosen race, what race would not have wished to be the chosen race; your race chosen among so many others

---

[1] *What did he do to you that you have chosen him?* A free quotation from Alfred de Vigny's poem: *Moïse,* in which Moses expostulates with the Almighty for having made him the leader of Israel. In the original, the line runs as follows: *Que vous ai-je donc fait pour être votre élu?* the implication being that to be chosen is in itself a form of punishment, but the romantic poet's meaning is, needless to say, far from Joan of Arc's.

among all the races; among the countless others; above the others; over the heads of all the countless others; what people would not have asked to be your people; what people would not have enjoyed being your people; chosen, by such a choice; at any price, Lord, at any temporal price, even at the price of this dispersal. You have chosen, you have selected, you have taken from among them, from ascension to ascension you have taken from among them the long line, the high, ascending line of prophets; and like a summit the last of all; the last of the prophets, the first of the saints; Jesus who was Jewish, a Jew among you; race that received the greatest grace; the grace that was refused to the whole Christian people; mystery of grace; chosen race; what was not given to the greatest saints; to the greatest saints of the Christian people, you have had it; and not only on earth; but in heaven itself and so to speak even more in heaven; for you Christian saints, great saints of Christendom; in your eternity you gaze upon Jesus only in his glory! and you Jews, singular Jews, singular people, unique people, first people you have looked at him in his misery. You have looked at him one time for all times, the time that counted. And his misery was your misery. His misery proper was your misery proper. He was a Jew, a simple Jew, a Jew like yourselves, a Jew among you. You have known him as one says of a man: I knew him in the old days. And in the meantime, our forefathers, our heathen grandfathers, our peasant grandfathers, our fathers and fathers of our fathers in this land went on tilling the soil; went on tilling this land; everything went on as usual, everything went on as if nothing had happened; they went on dressing vines and growing wheat, but neither that vine nor that wheat had yet been used for any consecration; neither that bread nor that wine had yet been consecrated; women went on baking bread; but it was solely a temporal bread, a bread made of temporal wheat, a bread made of wheat from the soil; a bread solely for the hunger of the body; and the wine too was a wine made solely of the vine of the soil; the maidens tended the sheep, the maidens went on spinning wool; all of them innocent, but all heathens, all hard-working, Hauviette, they were already at work, they never ceased working. They went on. They were good people, they were poor people, but they didn't know. Their work was but a temporal work. Their work was but a work of the soil. They did not know what was being prepared. They had no idea, those good people, of the good tidings that had come, that had come from the country of the Jews. They had no idea. And they were informed just a little time after that. So that we too we are brothers of Jesus in our eternity. And in our time we were his brothers, we are his brothers in Adam, in our father Adam; we are brothers of Jesus in our humanity. But you, Jews, you were his brothers in his own family. Brothers of his race and of his lineage. Upon you did he shed tears that were unique. Upon yourselves did he weep on that multitude. You saw the color of his eyes; you heard the sound of his words. Of the same lineage for all eternity. You heard the very sound of his voice. Like little brothers, you have huddled up in the heat, in the mild warmth of his look. You have taken shelter, you have taken cover under the kindness of his look. Upon yourselves did he take pity on the crowd.

65

Jesus, Jesus, will you ever be present to us in that
way. If you were here, Lord, things just wouldn't
happen the way they are happening now. They never
would have happened that way.

MADAME GERVAISE
(Both of them in a vision.)

He is here.

He is here as on the first day.

He is here among us as on the day of his death.

He is here forever among us just as much as on the
first day.

Forever every day.

He is here among us all the days of his eternity.

His body, that same body of his, hangs on the same
cross;

His eyes, those same eyes of his, quiver with the
same tears;

His blood, that same blood of his, bleeds from the
same wounds;

His heart, that same heart of his, bleeds with the
same love.

The same sacrifice causes the same blood to flow.

A parish shone with an everlasting brightness, but
all the parishes shine eternally, for in all the parishes
there is the body of Jesus Christ.

The same sacrifice crucifies the same body, the same
sacrifice causes the same blood to flow.

The same sacrifice offers up the same flesh, the same
sacrifice sheds the same blood.

66

The same sacrifice sacrifices the same flesh and the same blood.

It is the same story, exactly the same, eternally the same, which happened in that time and in that country and which happens on all days in all days of all eternity.
In all the parishes of all Christendom.

Whether it be in Lorraine, whether it be in France,
All the market towns are bright in God's eyes,
All the market towns are Christian under God's gaze.

Jews, you do not realize your happiness; Israel, Israel, you do not realize your happiness; but you too, Christians, you too do not realize your happiness; your present happiness; which is the same happiness.
Your everlasting happiness.

Israel, Israel, you do not realize your greatness; but you too, Christians, you do not realize your greatness; your present greatness; which is the same greatness.
Your everlasting greatness.

(Pointing to all the market towns, parishes, steeples in the valley, Domremy, Maxey, Vaucouleurs, and in them as well as beyond them to all the market towns, all the parishes, all the steeples of Christendom.)

All the market towns are loved under God's gaze,
All the market towns are Christian, all the market towns are sacred,
All the market towns are under God's gaze.

(As if, at last, taking notice of each other.)

JEANNETTE

Good morning, Madame Gervaise.

MADAME GERVAISE

Good morning, my daughter. May Jesus the Saviour save your soul forever.

JEANNETTE

Amen, Madame Gervaise. Did my uncle tell you that I wanted to see you?

MADAME GERVAISE

Yes, daughter, and I had an idea that you were unhappy.

JEANNETTE

Alas.

MADAME GERVAISE

God leads us, my child, God leads us by the hand. We are in God's hand. We do nothing but what God allows and wishes. It is God, God himself who led me this morning to you.

JEANNETTE

Amen, Madame Gervaise.

MADAME GERVAISE

God led me to you because you were unhappy. Here in the parish, they imagine that you are pleased with your life because you are a good Christian, because you are a good parishioner, because you are devout; because you made a good first communion; because you attend mass well, and vespers too; because you go to church often; and because in the

68

fields you kneel at the distant sound of peaceful bells.

JEANNETTE

Alas.

MADAME GERVAISE

I know that all that is not enough. I had an idea you too were unhappy, and that is why I came right away.

(A pause.)

I know. I know that you have on the contrary experienced all the sadness of a Christian soul. And that is infinite sadness.

(A pause.)

I have gone through that. The saints, all the saints have gone through that. It is the very condition, the hard condition, the hard law, the hard apprenticeship of holiness. I too have gone through that, I unworthy. You in your turn are going through it. Everyone in his turn. Everyone at his hour. God works on us when he wishes. God works on each of us in his turn. You are not the first one. You will not be the last one.

JEANNETTE

(As if attacking her. Suddenly.)

Do you know, Madame Gervaise, that the soldiers are everywhere storming the market towns and breaking into churches?

MADAME GERVAISE

(At first as if compelled to defend herself.)

I know it, daughter.

69

JEANNETTE

Do you know that they feed their horses oats on the venerable altar?

MADAME GERVAISE

I know it, daughter. And they said that it made a very good manger, a very convenient manger, just at the right height for the horses' heads.

JEANNETTE

And that they say dreadful things to the Blessed Virgin, to our mother the Holy Virgin; and that they insult, and that they blaspheme Jesus on his cross.

And it seems that once they even struck the face of Jesus on his cross.

MADAME GERVAISE

That is not the first time he was struck in the face. And our sins strike him in the face outrageously every day.

Our sins insult him and strike him in the face every day.

JEANNETTE

Do you know, Madame Gervaise, and may the good Lord ever forgive me for having dared to say these words in your hearing, do you know that the soldiers drink out of the very holy chalices the wine that makes them drunk?

MADAME GERVAISE

I know it, daughter.

JEANNETTE

Must I, Lord, must I say this also to you. Must I in order to put an end to . . .

MADAME GERVAISE

. . . In order to consummate this distress . . .

JEANNETTE

Must I also say this to you? Do you know that they feast on the very holy consecrated host?

MADAME GERVAISE

All the saints have gone through that. We unworthy ones, we lowly ones, we small ones we go through it. I have gone through it, you are going through it, we shall all go through it. And yet we people are people of small account.

JEANNETTE

The blood of Jesus, the vessel, the chalice that contains the blood of Jesus.

MADAME GERVAISE

They tear down houses; they tear down churches.

One house torn down, one house built; one house torn down, the same house rebuilt; one house torn down, another house built; one old house torn down we will build, we will always rebuild new houses; there will never be lacking stones of the earth to build new houses; new earthly houses; and our arms will never fail, our arms will not fail us to build temporal houses, to set up houses of this earth.

What of it, we will always rebuild enough new houses.

We will build enough temporal houses.

JEANNETTE

The blood of Jesus, the blood of Jesus.

MADAME GERVAISE

They tear down our houses; were they to tear down all we have, if it please God, we will have in the house of our father a house which soldiers will never tear down.

JEANNETTE

The body of Jesus, the body of Jesus. That they desecrate the bread and the wine, the body and the blood of Jesus.

MADAME GERVAISE

We have other houses than the houses we have. We have houses which the soldiers will not get at.

A house which the soldiers will not tear down.

We have other houses, we have other houses.

There are other houses than our father's house. There is another father than our own father. God has prepared for us, Jesus has won for us other mansions, Jesus has won for us eternal mansions.

We have another father than the father we have.

JEANNETTE

The body of Jesus, the sacred body of Jesus.

MADAME GERVAISE

They tear down the churches. We will always build new ones. We will always rebuild stone churches.

There is another father than our father.

We will always rebuild temporal churches. We will always set up perishable churches.

But there is a church which they shall not get at. There is a church of God which they shall not get at. There is a church in heaven, in God's heaven. There is a Church eternal. Which they shall not get at.

The saints have been won forever, the saints are saints forever, eternally forever. Nothing can ever more send the saints to perdition. Jesus is won forever. Jesus is holy, he is Jesus forever, eternally forever. And in God's heaven there is a body of Jesus which the fingers of sinful hands will never touch again, never again in eternity.

A body of Jesus which the fingers of sinful hands will never again desecrate.

JEANNETTE

The body of Jesus. To use for sin itself the body itself, the sacred body of Jesus.

MADAME GERVAISE

There is another Church than all the churches *(pointing to them)* of the Meuse and of Lorraine, other than Domremy and Maxey, than Vaucouleurs and Nancy, than Reims and Rouen, than Paris and than Rome. There is a heavenly Rome. There is a heavenly Jerusalem. There is another Church than all the churches of the earth. There is another Church than all the churches of Christendom itself. There is a Church which sinful hands will not tear down, will never in eternity pollute. There is another Church than all the churches of all the land of Christendom.

JEANNETTE

And yet when those Roman soldiers dared to touch your perishable body, your imperishable body, at least they did not know that you were the son of God. But these, Christians, Christian soldiers, baptized in their parishes by the curés of their parishes through the care of their fathers and mothers assisted by their

73

godfathers and godmothers, these insult you, knowing who you are; these desecrate you, knowing who you are, desecrate your body. Verily, Lord, they are at their wits' end, they don't know what further evil to imagine; sins are now committed which had never been committed. People are at their wits' end.

Sins which one would not suspect.

MADAME GERVAISE

I know it, daughter.

And I know that damnation rises like a swelling tide in which souls are drowned.

And I know that your soul is sorrowful unto death, when you see the everlasting, the increasing and everlasting damnation of souls.

JEANNETTE

Do you know, Madame Gervaise, that we, who see all this going on under our eyes and are content at present with empty charities . . .

MADAME GERVAISE

Child, child, child, charities are never empty.

JEANNETTE

. . . and without wanting to kill war . . .

MADAME GERVAISE

My child, my poor child, my child, my little child, you do not speak like a little girl, you do not speak like a little Christian.

Above all, don't be angry. That is also a great sin.

JEANNETTE

. . . content at present with empty charities, since

74

we do not want to kill war, are accomplices in all this? We who let the soldiers do as they wish, do you know that we too torment bodies and damn souls? We too, even we, strike crucified Jesus on the cheek. We too, even we, profane the imperishable body of Jesus.

(A pause.)

Accomplice, accomplice, it's like author. We are accomplices in this, we are the authors of this. Accomplice, accomplice, it is just as if you said author.

He who allows things to be done is like him who orders them to be done. It is all one. It goes together. And he who allows things to be done, just like him who orders them to be done, it is altogether like him who does them. *(As if about to rise.)* It is worse than him who does them. Because he who does shows courage, at least, in doing. He who commits a crime has at least the courage to commit it. And when you allow the crime to be committed, you have the same crime, and cowardice to boot. Cowardice on top of it all.

There is everywhere infinite cowardice.

An accomplice, an accomplice, that is worse than being the author, infinitely worse.

MADAME GERVAISE

I know, daughter, that you are, all of you, the damners of souls. And I know that your soul is sorrowful unto death, from knowing that it is an accomplice of universal Evil; accomplice and author, you confess it; accomplice and author of universal Evil; accomplice and author of Sin; accomplice and author of this universal perdition, and you feel desperately fainthearted.

(A pause.)

But that is nothing yet.
It is nothing.

(A long pause.)

Daughter, forgive the words that I shall now dare to utter; I am but a poor woman; I have seen such a lot of things too, in my childhood, when I was a little girl. Like you. Just as you are now. They think that they have said everything when they have said: She has gone to a convent. One never talks enough. And one never talks soon enough. One never talks enough to one's friends. Nor soon enough. All the more to one's bosom friends. I had rather offend and help you; before God; than not to offend, and to betray you. I must offend you, if need be. Forgive me the words which I shall now dare to utter; afterwards, I shall go away, if you wish, without ever seeing you again.

(A brief pause.)

I know too your new sorrow; I know the sorrow which to you seems frightful beyond all sorrow, frightful even beyond all imagining; why you called me; why I came.

(A brief pause.)

To despise oneself, one would even despise oneself, one would get used to it, become accustomed to it; there exist, there are worse habits: You have experienced how fainthearted are those you have loved, . . . those you have loved . . .

(Jeannette makes a gesture.)

Those you love, those you love, those you love, daughter, my poor child.

(The gesture of rebellion subsides.)

You are right, daughter, my poor child.

Child, child, one loves always. But to love those one despises is very much of a good deed. But to despise those one loves, that is the greatest sorrow there is.

Those one would like to honor, and one should honor, and wants to honor. Whom one honors. Just the same.

That is the basest and most unworthy deed.

You have experienced that all those you have loved are cowardly, you have experienced that your father is cowardly; that your mother is cowardly.

(Jeannette hangs her head.)

Your father, that big strong man who is afraid of nothing, save God, who is such a good Christian; your mother, who is such a good Christian, who goes on pilgrimages; and your brothers, and your big sister, and your friends.

(In a calling up of the past.)

I too have had friends.
I too had friends.

(Proceeding afresh.)

Mengette, whom I saw this morning; Hauviette, who does not want to see me;

(With a shake of her head as Jeannette makes a gesture.)

I know, I know. *(Dryly and at the same time with great sadness.)* No, she does not want to. You have experienced how cowardly they all are, and accomplices of universal Evil; accomplices, authors of Sin; accomplices, authors of this universal perdition; and they are therefore responsible for it. Accountable. Responsible for the souls that damn themselves to those very souls, and responsible to God, for souls belong to him, and you allow them to damn themselves without doing anything, and you damn yourselves in letting souls of God damn themselves.

(A pause.)

And so then we have an enumeration and an endless unfolding of damnations, an explanation for endless damnations; a linking together, a dreadful dance of perditions; one dragging the other along, inevitable; one drags the other along in this infernal round; one holds the other by the hand like a dreadful sister; and they hold each other by a hand that will never let go. One holds the other, the other holds one, one holds on to the other and one strengthens the other. Every day something new is invented. Every day some unknown thing is imagined. New damnations, redoublings of damnation, the circles of hell unfolding below circles.

(A pause.)

You lie.

Since you have known that, you have been a liar; you have lied to your father, lied to your mother, to your brothers, to your big sister, to your friends,

78

because you pretend to love them, and you cannot love them. And yet you love them just the same. You lie to yourself, because you want to make yourself believe that you love them, and you cannot love them. And you do love them just the same.

You do not love them and yet you do.

You love them just the same. With what love. How can you love them. With a love that is a lie, a love betrayed and betraying itself, perpetually betraying itself, a love that is warped. All uprightness is henceforth distorted, all uprightness is now crooked. You lie by the sound of your voice. You lie by the look in your eyes. All is forever warped in your soul. And all is forever warped in your life; warped is filial love and warped brotherly love; filial love, the first of blessings; after God's blessings; among God's blessings; warped is friendship; warped is filial love; warped friendship's love, warped your own friendships; warped all your feelings: Your whole life is a lie and a sham. And you live in your house, with your people, and you feel more irreparably alone and unhappy than a motherless child.

(Deep silence.)

One hope remained for you. You were going on for twelve. In this great distress, you at least expected, you said to yourself that it would soon end, for you were nearing the communication of the body of Our Lord, you were as close as possible to the communication of the body of Our Lord, and the communication of the body of Our Lord cures all evils.

(Deep silence.)

The hour is come, the hour that was awaited; the

awaited hour, the hour that was made ready since all eternity.

The hour you awaited for days and days, the hour you awaited since your baptism, the hour you awaited since all eternity. Since your eternity.

The day is come, the great day, you have received communication of the body of Our Lord.

In your turn, after thousands and thousands and hundreds of thousands of others, after hundreds and thousands of thousands of Christian women; in your turn, a Christian and a parishioner, like so many and so many Christian women, like so many and so many parishioners, like so many saints themselves, in your turn you have received the body of Our Lord Jesus Christ, the same body of Our Lord Jesus Christ.

After fourteen centuries, your turn it is to receive. Your turn to draw near.

In your turn you received for the first time the body of Our Lord Jesus Christ.

Long expected day. Day of endless mourning, for the communication of the body of Our Lord cures all evils; and you were once more with yourself that evening; and you were alone; and you had received the same body, the same as the saints had received; and the communication of the body of Our Lord cures all evils; and God had come; and that evening you found yourself once more alone in the same situation; but it was not the same, it was infinitely worse; you found yourself once more in the same sorrow; it was not the same, it was infinitely worse, it had become infinite; you found yourself once more in the same distress; the same, the same, alas; but it was not the same; it had become infinitely worse, it had become infinite, it had turned into something else; for the greatest physician in the world had gone by, and had not changed anything.

The same solitude. In the same solitude. And it was not the same.

It was no longer before. It was after. The evening of your day. Before, it was a great distress. But it was only a distress awaiting its remedy. After, it was a great distress no longer awaiting its remedy. It was a great distress over which the remedy had passed. In vain. The same distress: a distress of another kind, infinitely different, infinitely worse; infinitely tried, infinitely verified; that had become infinite; since the only remedy in the world had passed over it and had not changed anything.

Of the same distress, starting from the same, remaining the same, changed, infinitely changed. Before, after.

For the evening hour is infinitely different from the same morning hour.

(Suddenly, almost brutally.)

Be that as it may, you had made a failure of your first communion.

(A pause. Darkly:)

It is almost worse than if one made a failure of one's judgment and of the day of one's death.

JEANNETTE
(A long pause.)

It is true.

It is true that my soul is sorrowful unto death; I am in distress; I never thought that the death of my soul could be so painful.

All those I loved are absent from myself.

MADAME GERVAISE
Even God. That's it, all of them.

JEANNETTE
All those I loved are absent from me.

MADAME GERVAISE
That's what damnation is; that's perdition itself.

JEANNETTE
All those I loved are absent from me: that is what killed me past all remedy . . .

MADAME GERVAISE
The only remedy there is in the world came, and the only physician; and the remedy did nothing for you; the physician did nothing for you; and the evening of this day, you found yourself in the same situation as in the morning.

JEANNETTE
Alas.

MADAME GERVAISE
Your life is a perpetual lie. And yet you had blessed that morning, that rising day; you had blessed that sun rising on the hillsides *(pointing to them in front of her)* on the hillsides of Lorraine, on the hillsides of the Meuse.

JEANNETTE
Alas, alas.

82

MADAME GERVAISE

The creature sun on the creature Meuse.

JEANNETTE

All those I love are absent from me; that is what killed me past all remedy; and I feel that my human death is soon to come.

I shall not go far. I can go no further. My life is all hollow within me.

MADAME GERVAISE

Woe to the heart which the body of Jesus has not filled; woe to the heart which the body of Jesus has not satiated.

JEANNETTE

I cannot, I cannot go further.

Oh, may my human death, Lord, come as soon as possible. O Lord I pity our human life from which those we love are forever absent.

MADAME GERVAISE

Child, have mercy on perdition; child, have mercy on life in hell where those who are damned and accursed, where those who are damned and lost undergo the worst pain; which is that God himself is absent from their eternity.

JEANNETTE

Oh, if in order to save from the eternal flame
The bodies of the dead who are damned and maddened by pain,
I must abandon my body to the eternal flame,
Lord, give my body to the eternal flame;

My body, my poor body, to that flame which will
    never be quenched.
My body, take my body for that flame.
My wretched body.
My body worth so little, counting for so little.
Of little weight.
My poor body of so little a price.

(A pause.)

And if to save from eternal Absence
The souls of the damned maddened by Absence,
I must abandon my soul to eternal Absence,
May my soul go to eternal Absence.

My soul to that absence that will never be quenched.

MADAME GERVAISE

Be still, sister: you have blasphemed: God, in his
infinite mercy, has kindly consented to the saving of
souls through human suffering; I say, human suffering; earthly suffering; militant suffering; not, of
course, suffering that suffers; certainly not, assuredly
in no wise the suffering of hell.

*(As if in protest against an impossibility: exclaiming
in the face of evidence:)*

For then they would not be *lost,* if their suffering
were not lost. For then the world would undergo the
same suffering as ours, it would be the same suffering,
as ours. For then they would be like us.

They would have grace.

Now they are not like us. There is a difference. An

immeasurable one. There is, there has been judgment.

Otherwise they would be like us. There are, there can be but two kinds, there can be but two races of suffering: the suffering that is not lost, and the suffering that is lost. We are of the suffering that is not lost, together with Jesus Christ; our suffering is of the same kind, it is of the same race as the suffering of Jesus Christ; our suffering is never lost, when we are willing.

All of us partake in suffering that is not lost, when we are willing, from Jesus to the last of Christians.

From Jesus himself to the last of sinners.

There is, there is elsewhere a suffering that is lost, that is quite lost; that is always lost, even if one weren't willing; whatever one wants; whatever they want; whatever they want eternally.

Whatever they do. Whatever they do eternally.

That's what hell is. Otherwise there would be no hell. It would be the same as with us; it would be the same thing everywhere.

Throughout the whole creation.

If their suffering could be of any use, my child, my poor child, they would be like us; they would be us; there would not be, there would never have been judgment. If their suffering could be of any use, as soon as suffering can be of any use, it couples itself to, it connects itself, it binds itself with the suffering of Jesus Christ. It becomes of the same race. It becomes, it becomes right away of the same kind, of the same race, of the same family as the suffering of Jesus Christ.

85

It becomes the sister of the suffering of Jesus Christ.

It becomes suffering in communion.

There would be no difference.

If their suffering were of any use, child, if it could be of any use, but then they would be in the communion.

And they are not in the communion.

All suffering that can be of any use, all suffering that is of any use is sister to the suffering of Jesus Christ; the daughter of God's suffering; the same as the suffering of Jesus Christ.

There would not have been judgment.

There is, elsewhere there is suffering that is of no use, that is eternally useless. That is always in vain, empty, that is always hollow, always useless, always sterile, always uncalled for, always therefore non chosen, all of it, eternally all of it, eternally forever, whatever they may wish.

Whatever they do. Whatever they do eternally.

Whatever there be.

Learn, child, learn what hell is.

There is the mark, there the distinction, there the difference. It is infinite.

Otherwise, if they served, they would be like us. *They would be as happy as we are.* They would be like Jesus on his cross. But we alone have the right to be like Jesus on his cross. We alone have the right to be in the image and likeness, in imitation of Jesus to suffer in the image and likeness; in imitation of Jesus. Among other things, they, unfortunates, have not even the right to be on a cross.

Too late, too late, after, it is too late.

There is: on earth, and that is all. After, it is no longer on earth.

There is the suffering on earth, and after, that's all.

Otherwise, they would not be dead, they would not be lost, they would not be damned, they would not be judged.

They would be men like us; they would be alive, earthly; they would be living people; they would be before the judgment. They wouldn't be after.

(A pause.)

Daughter, daughter, there are many Churches; in the Church. But there is only one. There is only one Church. There are several Churches. There is the Church militant, in which we are. There is the suffering Church, in which we may avoid being; if it please God. There is the Church triumphant, where we ask to be. If it please God. But there is no Church in hell.

There is not a Church of hell.

It is sheer madness. An absurd imagination. It is inconceivable.

All three are living Churches; there is not, there cannot be a dead Church.

The Church is essentially, substantially alive. It perpetually receives life from God, Jesus has promised it eternal life. It is naturally, supernaturally alive. There is not, there cannot be a dead Church.

If their suffering could be of any use, was of any use, they would be a Church, they would be in the Church.

Militant, suffering, triumphant, all three alive, there is not, there cannot be a dead Church.

(A pause.)

There is the Church militant; we belong to it; it is the Church of soldiers in a certain way; we belong to it; everybody goes through it, everybody has gone through it; we know what we have to do in it.

We go through it. Everybody has to see service in it, to see service for a certain time.

Service that does not have to be renewed.

One doesn't re-enlist.

After, one is divided.

There is the suffering Church. We must try, we must ask not to belong to it. That is the law; that is the rule. For them, for them we can usefully, we must multiply our work, our prayers, our sufferings. Our merits, if it be allowed to filch that word from Jesus Christ. To merits only. To the merits of Jesus Christ. There, perhaps, are our fathers and the fathers of our fathers. God rest their souls. To work for them, to pray for them, to suffer for them. To acquire merit for them. That is the law; that is the rule. And it is not necessary to ask it of us; it is not necessary to order us to do it. Nor to compel us to do it, nor even to advise us to do it. It is our impulse, something we do of our own accord; it is our love itself; it is communion itself.

It is done by our love of its own accord, through a natural impulse of our love.

By our human love, our family love, our filial love.

There is a Church triumphant. We must try to

belong to it. No use concealing that. No use trying
to be modest about it. We must try, we must ask to
belong to it. That is the law, that is the rule. Common
to all. We must pray to them, and in the meantime
we must pray to them for others and for us, no use
concealing it, we must pray to them, for others in the
suffering Church and for others in the Church militant, for others on earth and for us and for others
elsewhere, ask for their intercession, ask them to in-
tercede for others and for us, for all those of the suffering Church and for all those of the Church militant. To be with them later on. Among them. To be
with them like them. It is not only the law and the
rule. It is also our impulse itself. It is also our love.
It is also communion itself. It is done of our own
accord.

It is done of our own accord, by the natural impulse of our love. The impulse of our charity.

Of our human love, of our family love, of our filial
love. Of our charity.

And there is yet this difference. And it is all-important. And it is all. That those of the suffering
Church are sure to go there. And that we are sure of
nothing. Since we are before.

Of nothing at all.

Since we have not yet decided.

Have not yet been directed.

Separated.

Set on the march towards one of the three ways.

On one of the three ways.

On one of the two roads.

Such is communion, such is the life of the three

living Churches. But there is no dead Church. There is no Church that would not communicate.

Which would not be a Church, which *therefore* would not be a Church. There is no dead Church.

(A pause.)

My child, my little girl, the good Lord has made cadres. We must work, we must pray, we must suffer in the cadres which the good Lord has made. He kindly consents to accept our sufferings here below for the salvation of souls in danger. But he did not want suffering in hell to be used for the salvation of souls; he would not accept our sufferings in that place yonder to save souls in danger. There is no dead Church.

JEANNETTE

(With simplicity.)

There is so much suffering then that is lost.

MADAME GERVAISE

Wretch, wretched child, how you do talk.

JEANNETTE

In creation there is so much created suffering that is lost.

MADAME GERVAISE

Suffering is not the point in question. If suffering were the only thing, who would not suffer. Who doesn't suffer.

(A pause.)

There is useful suffering and useless suffering. There is fruitful suffering and unfruitful suffering.

(A pause.)

That is why our master, the master of all of us . . .

JEANNETTE

Our Lord, Our Lord Jesus Christ.

MADAME GERVAISE

Our master of mastery, of all mastery, of one and the other mastery; our master of seigniory and our master of teaching; our master of domination and our master of apprenticeship.

JEANNETTE

Our Lord, Our Lord Jesus.

MADAME GERVAISE

He must have known, he did. It was his business. To save. It was his office. He must have known. He was our saving master. That is why our master, the master of us all; the son of man versed in giving his suffering, kindly consented, in order to save our souls, to give all suffering, worth giving, including the valid suffering of temptation, but never went so far as to give empty suffering, even that of sin. The Saviour kindly consented to give all human suffering; it was in the contract, it was in the covenant. He had made himself man. His suffering also made itself human, completely human. But he did not consent to damn himself; and it is sheer madness, it is inconceivable, it is absurd; it would be blasphemy, committing infinite blasphemy even to entertain such a fancy: it would be committing unheard-of sacrilege; for he knew that his suffering in hell, even his, that his suffering in hell could not be of any use for our salvation.

It is madness to have that thought.

Even to have that thought. To see it only passing through one's own mind.

It is a very great impiety. It is a great temptation. It is more than impiety.

It is an unbelievable temptation.

An awful blasphemy.

JEANNETTE

Can it be that so much suffering is lost.

MADAME GERVAISE

It is an awful mystery, child, *(as if making a confession:)* the greatest mystery in creation. It is a greater mystery than Incarnation itself and than Redemption, than the mystery of Incarnation and than the mystery of Redemption. As for the Passion of Jesus, at least you see what good that did. And the whole of Incarnation is made clear by the whole of Redemption.

JEANNETTE

If then to save from the flame eternal
The bodies of the dead that are damned and go mad
    with suffering,
I must long abandon my body to human suffering,
Lord, keep my body for human suffering;
    And if to save from eternal Absence
The souls of the damned going mad because of Absence,
I must long abandon my body to human suffering.
Let it remain alive in human suffering.

MADAME GERVAISE

Be still, sister, you have blasphemed:
For if the son of man, in his very last hour,

Cried out louder than a lost soul in his dreadful anguish,
With a cry that rang as untrue as a divine blasphemy,
It was because the Son of God knew.

One wonders why he should have uttered that dreadful cry. One wonders, had it been otherwise.

All the statements are positive, at that moment he uttered a dreadful cry.

So one wonders why at that moment he should have uttered that dreadful cry.

On the contrary. He should have been pleased.

It was over.

It was done.

All was finished.

His passion was at an end; his incarnation was as it were at an end; achieved; his passion was completed; achieved; redemption was completed; achieved.

There was nothing left (for him) but that formality: death.

Redemption was completed and crowned;
Crowned with thorns, the supreme crown.

It was at that moment that he should; that he ought to have been happy.

O best beloved son who went back to his father;
Son of tender love who went up again to heaven;
Son among all sons who went home to his father,
Prodigal child, son prodigal of his blood;
O best beloved son who went up to his father.

One wonders why he should have cried out at that moment. He had precisely begun to make an end.

He had served his time of humanity;
He was leaving the prison for the home of glory;
He was returning to his father's house.

Like a traveler at the last hours of his journey,
He had finished his journey on earth;
He had ended his journey to Jerusalem.

Like a tired traveler at the last hours of his journey,
He saw his home.

And like a reaper at the end of his day,
In both his father's hands he poured out his pay;
Like a tired reaper at the end of his harvest;
In both his father's hands he poured out his pay,
The souls of the just he had redeemed,
The pay he had so hardly earned.
The souls of the saints he had sanctified.
The souls of the just he had justified.
And the souls of sinners that he had justified with one
and the other hand.
That he had picked up like an ear of grain on the
ground.
That he had justified by his merits.

The souls of the just that he had earned like a day
laborer.
Like a poor journeyman working on farms.
Like a poor workman who hurries up with his work.
All he had stored up.
All the souls he had been able to gather by working
hard.
A big armful.

94

As much as both his hands could hold.
By not wasting any time.
Because it was his boss's time.
It belonged to his father who was his boss.
All he could hold in his arms.
In his eternal arms.
The souls of the just he had made fragrant with his
    virtues.
A full sheath, a whole potful; a whole sheathful, a
    whole armful, a whole bunch of souls.
As many as he could hold in his two hands.
As many as he could hold in his two arms.

He was like a son at the last hours of his day;
His father was waiting for him to embrace him at last;
An eternal kiss would lave his unsullied side;
A fatherly kiss would lave his unsullied brow;
An eternal kiss from his father would lave his smart-
    ing wounds,
Would refresh his smarting wounds,
And his head, and his side, and his feet, and his hands.
An eternal spring, pure eternal water awaited his
    smarting wounds.

A never-ending kiss would alight on his side;
A fatherly kiss would descend on his brow.

He was leaving his earthly home for his heavenly
    home;
The temporal home for the eternal home.

He was then about to return to his eternity.
The task was over and the work was done.

He had served his time of humanity.
The angels awaited him to celebrate his day.
The angels awaited him to lave his smarting wounds.
The angels awaited him to bathe his smarting wounds.
To stanch his wounds.
To dress his wounds.
The angels awaited him to wash his wounds.
The angels awaited him to bathe his wounds.
To stanch his smarting wounds.
Five dressings for the five Wounds.
With extra fine linen.
Made of flax.
But linen somewhat used.
Because it is softer.
An eternal spring to bathe his wounds.

The angels awaited him as he left our hands
To acclaim his name and sing his praise;
To wash his side; to wash his hands;
The angels awaited him to bathe him, to wash his
    wounds;
And the blood of his hands and the blood of his feet.
And the nails of his hands, and the nails of his feet.

As he had washed the feet of his disciples.
So the angels would wash his feet.
The master's feet.
And not only the feet.
But as Peter had asked.
Simon Peter.
Not the feet only, but also the hands and the head.
But when he had washed his disciples' feet.
It was in a well-closed room.

96

A really quiet one.
In the room where they had supper.
Still quiet and well closed.
And at the present time it would be in heaven.
Now it would be in heaven.
From now on.
   The spirits were waiting for him after the death of
      bodies.
And the pure spirits, pure after the bodies of flesh.
And the subtle spirits, pure after carnal death, after
   gross death.
And the subtle spirits, pure after the gross bodies.

Strange mystery.
The spirits waited for him to wash his body.
As if they knew about bodies.
As if they knew what a body was.
As if it concerned them.
Strange mystery.

One sees very well that it was his own body.

   His seat awaited him at the right of the father.
   He was the dauphin ascending towards the king.

   As he was going to return to his eternity,
On the point of returning into his eternity,
It is then all the statements agree, all the statements
   are positive, it is then he uttered that awful cry.

As he trod again into his eternity.
After years and years, after centuries and centuries,
one single action.
Made ready the home of maternal glory.

After a long journey entered his home.

After so many battles an eternal peace;
After so much of war an eternal victory;
After so much misery an eternal glory;
After so much loneliness an eternal exaltation;
After so much contesting, an uncontested reign.

You understand. It was over. He was going home.
He was returning to his home. All he had to do was
to go back home. He was going away from here. He
saw from afar his father's house. He saw other houses
around here.
The other house, his foster father's house.

He saw once more the lowly cradle of his childhood,
In which his body was laid for the first time;
The swaddling clothes on the straw and the ox and
the ass' belly and the gifts, the shepherds and the
kings.

JEANNETTE

He was born in Bethlehem in a poor stable.

MADAME GERVAISE

The gifts which the shepherds and kings had
brought him.
He saw once more the lowly cradle at Bethlehem
In which his body was laid for the first time;

98

The gifts which the shepherds and kings had made him, were making him.

Bethlehem, Bethlehem, and you Jerusalem.
Life begun at Bethlehem and finished at Jerusalem.
Life included between Bethlehem and Jerusalem.
Life inscribed between Bethlehem and Jerusalem.
He saw once more the lowly cradle of his childhood.

Life begun at Bethlehem and not ending at Jerusalem.

The swaddling clothes on the straw waiting to be washed;
Another set of swaddling clothes was ready for the change.
The shepherds falling down before him offered wool.

Wool from their sheep, child; wool from the sheep of those days.
Wool like what we spin.

JEANNETTE

Wool like this.

MADAME GERVAISE

The wise kings offered gold, incense and myrrh. Gold as to their king.

JEANNETTE

Incense as to their God.

MADAME GERVAISE

Myrrh as to a mortal man.

JEANNETTE

Who one day would be embalmed.

99

MADAME GERVAISE

The wise kings Gaspar, Melchior and Balthasar.

JEANNETTE

Gaspar and Balthasar and Melchior the wise kings.

MADAME GERVAISE

All that took place in the light of heaven;
The angels had formed into choirs in the night.
The angels sang like flowers in the night.
Above the shepherds, above the wise kings
The angels in the night sang everlastingly.

Under the kindness of heaven, under its youthful-
ness, under its eternity.
Of the firmament he called heaven.

Like song flowers, like hymn flowers, like prayer flowers, like grace flowers.

Like a flowering, like a leafing, like a fruition of
prayer and grace.

All that took place below the angel choirs.
All that took place below the kindness of heaven.
The star in the night shone like a gold nail.
The star in the night shone everlastingly,
The star in the night shone like a gold pin.

JEANNETTE

A star had appeared, a star had risen which will
then never again show itself.

MADAME GERVAISE

Like all little children he played with pictures.

Cry still ringing in all humanity;
Cry that made the Church militant totter;
In which the suffering Church too recognized its own
    fear;
Through which the Church triumphant experienced
    its triumph;
Cry ringing at the heart of all humanity;
Cry ringing at the heart of all Christendom;
O culminating cry, everlastingly valid.

Cry as if God himself had sinned like us;
As if God himself had despaired;
O culminating cry, everlastingly valid.

As if even God had sinned like us.
Committing the greatest sin.
Which is to despair.
The sin of despair.

Louder than the two thieves hanging beside him;
And who howled at death like famished dogs.
The thieves howled but a human howl;
The thieves howled but a cry of human death;
Also they slavered but human slaver:

The Just One alone uttered the everlasting cry.

But why? What was the matter with him?

The thieves uttered but a human cry;

For they knew but human distress;

They had experienced but human distress.

He alone could utter the superhuman cry;
He alone then knew that superhuman distress.

That is why the thieves uttered only a cry that was quenched in the night.

And he uttered the cry that will sound forever, eternally forever, the cry that will eternally never be quenched.

In any night. In any night of time and eternity.

For the thief on the left and the thief on the right
Felt only the nails in the hollow of their hands.

What mattered to him the thrust of the Roman spear;
What mattered to him the strain of nails and the hammer;
The piercing of nails, the piercing of the spear;
What mattered to him the nails in the hollow of the hand;
The piercing of nails in the hollow of both his hands;

His aching throat.
Smarting.
Burning.
Tearing apart.
His parched throat all athirst.
His parched gorge.
His gorge athirst.
His left hand that burned.
And his right hand.

His left foot that burned.
And his right foot.
Because his left hand was pierced.
And his right hand.
And his left foot was pierced.
And his right foot.
All of his four limbs.
His poor four limbs.
And his side that burned.
His pierced side.
His pierced heart.
And his heart that burned.
His heart consumed with love.
His heart devoured with love.

Peter's denial and the Roman spear;
The spitting, the insults, the crown of thorns;
The scourging reed, the scepter made of a reed;
The shouts of the people and the Roman tormentors.
The blow on his face. For it was the first time he had
     been struck in the face.

   He had not cried out under the Roman spear;
He had not cried out under the kiss of perjury;
He had not cried out under the storm of abuse;
He had not cried out under the Roman tormentors.

He had not cried out under the bitterness of ingrati-
     tude.
The bitter taste in his throat.
In his gorge.
His throat made dry and bitter by bitterness.

Dry from choking down bitterness.
Dry, bitter from choking down ingratitude.
Men's ingratitude.
Bitter, suffocating from choking down.
Suffocated by floods of ingratitude.
Strangled by choking down.
And he would no longer speak in similes.

He had not cried out in the face of perjury;
He had not cried out in the face of abuse;
He had not cried out in the face of the Roman tor-
  mentors.
So why did he cry out; before what did he cry out.

Tristis, tristis usque ad mortem;
Sorrowful unto death; but unto what death;
Unto dying; or unto that moment
Of death.

Once more he saw the lowly cradle of his childhood,
The crèche,
In which his body was laid for the first time;
He foresaw the spacious tomb for his dead body,
The last cradle of every man,
In which every man must lie down.
To sleep.
Supposedly.
Apparently.
To rest at last.
To rot.
His body.
Between four boards.
Awaiting the resurrection of bodies.

Until the resurrection of bodies.
Happy when the souls don't rot.

And he was a man;
He was to undergo the common lot;
To lie down there like everybody;
He had to go through it like everybody;
He would have to go through it.
Like the others.
Like everybody.
Like so many others.
After so many others.
His body would lie for the last time.
But he would stay there only two days, three days;
    because of resurrection.
For he would rise again the third day.
Because of his particular resurrection and of his as-
    cension.
His own.
Which he had made with his own body, with the same
    body.

The linen of his burial;
As white as the handkerchief of that famous Veronica;
The linen as white as swaddling clothes.
And which one winds around exactly like swaddling
    clothes.
But bigger, much bigger.
He had become a man.
He was a child who had grown much.

The big white sheet of his burial.
He would be buried by those women.

Piously by the hands of those women.
Like a man who has died in a village.
Quietly in his house in his village.
Having received the last sacraments.

Piously buried and quietly, by those women.
Without being disturbed by anyone.
By the pious hands of those women.
By the pious fingers of those women.
That is what would be called the descent from the
	cross.
Because the Romans weren't bad.
All those Romans.
They were not bad at heart.
They wouldn't quarrel with his hanging body.
His body that had been unhanged.
They wouldn't torment his remains.
His mortal remains.
They wouldn't try to pick a quarrel with those poor
	women.
The holy women.
Nor with that old Joseph of Arimathea.
That good old fellow.
That wise good old fellow.
Who would lend him his sepulchre.
You can lend each other many things during life.
One another.
In your household.
You can lend your donkey to go marketing.
You can lend your tub to do the washing in.
And your paddle.
You can lend your saucepan.
And your caldron.

And your pot to boil the soup in.
For the children.
For the whole household.
But to lend your sepulchre.
That's unusual.
To lend your sepulchre.
Your own tomb.
That old fellow would lend him his sepulchre.
That wise old fellow.
That shrewd old fellow.
That rich man.
That old shrewd one.
That man with a white beard.
With completely white hair.
That old sage.
That completely white man.
The sepulchre which he had had made.
Which he had had made for himself.
Since God the Father had so decided.
That the young died often before the old.
And that there were so many old people who didn't
   die.
And that he died in the lean youth of his three and
   thirty years.

When the even was come.
There came a rich man of Arimathea.
Named Joseph.
Who also himself was Jesus' disciple.

He went to Pilate.
Because some day or other you always have to ask
   men in power for something.

When you are alive, you defy them.
The hero, the saint, the martyr defy them.
But when you are dead.
Other people don't defy them for you when it comes
    to burials.
That shows that this Joseph of Arimathea was not
    afraid of going to men in power.
To have a talk with men in power.
He knew how to speak. He knew how to talk.
Evidently he was a man who knew how to talk.
He wasn't afraid of talking.
He knew what to say.
He wasn't afraid.
Even to Pilate.
He knew how to present himself.

He went to Pilate.
And begged the body of Jesus.
Then Pilate commanded the body to be delivered.

It was no more difficult than that.
When all is told, that Pilate wasn't a bad man.
He was an official.
A prefect.
A Roman prefect.
He had nothing in particular against Jesus.
He had nothing against the body of Jesus.
The next day he didn't even give it a thought.
He had no personal grudge against Jesus.
He had no grudge against the body of Jesus.
He had other matters to think about.
The next day he didn't even give it a thought.
And all humanity thinks of it forever.

108

And when Joseph had taken the body.
He wrapped it in a white winding sheet.
A clean winding sheet.
In sindone munda.
In a white winding sheet.

And he laid it in his own new tomb.
In his new sepulchre.
Posuit illud. He laid it.
Which he had hewn out of the rock.
In the rock.
And he rolled a great stone.
He rolled a great rock.
To the door of the sepulchre.
To the entrance of the sepulchre.
And departed.

One likes to think that afterwards he looked for another sepulchre for his own body.

The great tomb of his burial.
The holy sepulchre.
The sepulchre of his great sepulture.

He had said to John: John, behold thy mother.
And behold thy son.
He did not mourn for John, Mary and Magdalen;
He left them but for a few years;
One day they would go up to his father's house;
Parting would be but for a human time.
All that were attached to him, all that came from
him, all that owed him something, owed that side
of him something, were but human.

A distant cradle, a crèche in a stable; beneath the chorus of songs; beneath the angel choir; beneath the calm but quivering wings, calm but fluttering angel wings.

Better than they he measured the greatness of the penalty;
They measured it but with a human eye;
Even the reprobate, even the thief who had just lost his soul
Were before him but human reprobates.

Touching eternity with his eye that was God's eye,
He was at the very end and here at the same time,
He was at the very end and then at the same time.

He was in the middle and simultaneously at one and the other end.

He alone.

Of all men.

With one look he grasped all of his human life,
Which thirty years with his family and three years in public
Had not fulfilled;

Which thirty years with his family and three with his disciples,
His new family,
That other family,

His family according to the flesh and his chosen family,
One and the other according to the flesh, one and the other chosen,
Both according to the flesh, both chosen,
Had not consummated;

Which thirty years of work and three years of prayers,
Thirty-three years of work, thirty-three years of prayers,
Had not brought to an end;
Thirty-three years of work, thirty-three years of prayer.

Which thirty years of carpentry and three years of the spoken word,
Thirty-three years of carpentry, thirty-three years of the spoken word, secret; public;
Had not exhausted.

For he had worked as a carpenter, that was his trade.
He worked as a carpenter, he carpentered.
In carpentry.
He was a woodworker.
He had even been a good workman.
As he had been a good everything.
He was a journeyman carpenter.
His father was a boss with a very small business.
He worked in his father's house.
He did his work at home.

He saw, he saw once again the workbench and the
    plane.
The workbench. The block on which you rest the
    piece of timber you split.
The saw and the jointer.
The fine curly chips, the fine wood shavings.
The pleasant odor of new wood.
Newly cut.
Newly fashioned.
Newly sawed.
And the fair color, and the fair odor,
And the fine color, and the fine odor.
Of wood when you take off the bark.
When you peel it.
Like fine fruit.
Like good fruit.
Which you would eat.
But it is the tools that eat it.
And the bark that parts from the wood.
That draws aside.
That peels off.
That comes off so delicately under the axe.
That smells so good and has such a fine brown color.
How he liked that trade.
He was made for that trade.
Surely.
The trade of cradles and coffins.
Which are so much alike.
Of tables and beds.
And also of other pieces of furniture.
Of all furniture.
Because you mustn't forget anybody.
You mustn't discourage anybody.

The trade of sideboards, wardrobes, chests of drawers.
Of bread hutches.
To put bread in.
Of wooden stools.
And the earth is but your footstool.
Because in those days joiners weren't yet separated
from carpenters.
All those who did wood work.
How he had liked work well done.
A well done job.

He had been a good workman.
A good carpenter.
As he had been a good son.
A good son to his mother Mary.
A nice good child.
Nice and docile.
Nice and dutiful.
Nice and obedient to his father and mother.
A child.
Such as all parents would like to have.
A good son to his father Joseph.
To his foster father Joseph.
The old carpenter.
The master carpenter.

As he had been a good son also to his father.
To his father who art in heaven.

As he had been a good comrade to his little comrades.
A good schoolmate.
A good playmate.
A good play companion.

A good fellow workman.
A good fellow carpenter.
Among all other fellows.
Fellow carpenters.
For all fellows.
Fellow carpenters.
As he had been a good poor man.
As he had been a good citizen.

He had been a good son to his father and mother.
Until the day when he had begun his mission.
His preaching.
A good son to his mother Mary.
Until the day when he had begun his mission.
A good son to his father Joseph.
Until the day when he had begun his mission.
In short all had gone very well.
Until the day when he had begun his mission.

He was generally liked.
Everybody liked him.
Until the day when he had begun his mission.
Comrades, friends, fellow workmen, authorities,
Citizens,
Father and mother,
Thought it was all right,
Until the day when he had begun his mission.

Comrades thought him a good comrade.
Friends a good friend.
Fellow workmen a good fellow.
Not proud.
Citizens thought him a good citizen.

114

His equals a good equal.
Until the day when he had begun his mission.
Citizens thought he was a good citizen.
Until the day when he had begun his mission.
Until the day when he had showed himself another
   citizen.
The founder, the citizen of another city.
For he was a citizen of the heavenly city.
And of the everlasting city.

The authorities thought it was all right.
Until the day when he had begun his mission.
The authorities considered he was a man of order.
A serious young man.
A quiet young man.
A young man with good habits.
Easy to govern.
Giving back to Caesar what is Caesar's.

Until the day when he had begun disorder.
Introduced disorder.
The greatest disorder in the world.
The greatest disorder there ever was in the world.
The greatest order there had been in the world.
The only order.
There had ever been in the world.

Until the day when he had gone out of his way.
And in going out of his way he had disturbed the
   world.
Until the day when he had showed himself.
The only Government of the world.
The Master of the world.

The only Master of the world.
And when he appeared to all.
When his equals plainly saw.
That he had no equal.
At that moment the world began to think that he was
    too great.
And to bother him.

And until the day when he undertook to render unto
    God what belongs to God.

He was a good son to his father and mother.
He was a good son to his mother Mary.
And his father and mother thought everything was all
    right.
His mother Mary thought it was all right.
She was happy, she was proud of having such a son.
Of being the mother of a son like hers.
Of such a son.
And she gloried perhaps a little in herself and she
    magnified God.
Magnificat anima mea.
Dominum.
Et exultavit spiritus meus.
Magnificat. Magnificat.
Until the day when he had begun his mission.
But since he had begun his mission.
Perhaps she no longer said *Magnificat.*
For the last three days she wept.
She wept and wept.
As no other woman has ever wept.
No woman.
That is what he had brought in to his mother.
No boy had ever cost his mother so many tears.

116

No boy had ever made his mother weep so much.
That is what he had brought in to his mother.
Since he had begun his mission.

Because he had begun his mission.
For the last three days she wept.
For the last three days, she wandered, she followed.
She followed the procession.
She followed the events.
She followed as you follow a funeral.
But it was a living man's funeral.
A man who was still alive.
She followed what went on.
She followed as if she had been part of the procession.
Of the ceremony.
She followed like a follower.
Like a servant.
Like one of those Roman weepers.
At Roman funerals.
As if it had been her profession.
To weep.
She followed like a poor woman.
Like a regular attendant in the procession.
Like a follower of the procession.
Like a servant.
Already like a regular attendant.
She followed like a pauper.
Like a beggar woman.
They who had never asked anyone for anything.
Now she asked for charity.
Without seeming to, she asked for charity.
Since without seeming to, without even knowing it,
     she asked for the charity of mercy.

Mercy of a kind.
A certain mercy.
Pietas.
That is what he had done to his mother.
Since he had begun his mission.
She followed, she wept.
She wept and wept.
All that women know is to weep.
You saw her everywhere.
In the procession and somewhat apart from the procession.
Under the porticoes, under the arcades, in drafty places.
In the temples, in the palaces.
In the streets.
In the yards and in the back yards.
And she had also gone up to Calvary.
She too had climbed up to Calvary.
Which is a steep mountain.
And she did not even feel that she was walking.
She did not even feel that her feet were carrying her.
She did not feel her legs under her.
She too had gone up her calvary.
She too had gone up and up.
In the mob, lagging a little behind.
Gone up to Golgotha.
On Golgotha.
On top.
Up to the top.
Where he was now crucified.
Nailed by his four limbs.
Like a night bird nailed to a barn door.
He the King of Light.

At the place called Golgotha.
That is to say the place of the Skull.
That is what he had made of his mother.
His motherly mother.
A woman in tears.
A pauper.
A pauper of distress.
A pauper in distress.
A sort of beggarwoman begging for mercy.
Since he had begun to fulfill his mission.
For three days she followed and followed.
Accompanied only by three or four women.
By those holy women.
Escorted, surrounded only by those few women.
By those few holy women.
By the holy women.
In a word.
Since they were forever to be thus named.
Who thus earned.
Who thus made sure their share of heaven.
And, to be sure, they would have a good place.
As good as the one they had at this moment.
Because they would have the same place.
For they would be as close to him as at this moment.
I mean that they would be as close to him as at this
    moment.
As at this very moment.
Forever as close as at this very moment.
Forever as close as in this moment of time.
Of time in Judea.
Forever as close in his glory.
As in his passion.
In the glory of his passion.

And all four of them together or perhaps a little more
    or less.
A little more a little less.
They always formed a little separate group.
A little procession behind the great procession.
Somewhat behind.
And people recognized them.
She wept and wept under a big linen veil.
A big blue veil.
Somewhat faded.
That is what he had made of his mother.
She wept as it will never be granted to weep.
As it will never be demanded
Of a woman to weep on earth.
Eternally never.
Of any woman.
That is what he had made of his mother.
Of a motherly mother.
What was strange was that everyone respected her.
People greatly respect the parents of the condemned.
They even said: *poor woman.*
And at the same time they struck at her son.
Because man is like that.
Man is made that way.
The world is like that.
Men are what they are and you will never be able to
    change them.
She did not know that on the contrary he had come
    to change man.
That he had come to change the world.
She followed, she wept.
And at the same time they were hitting her boy.
She followed and followed.

Men are like that.

You can't change them.

You can't make them over.

You can never make them over.

And he had come to change them.

To make them over.

To change the world.

To make it over.

She followed, she wept.

Everybody respected her.

Everybody pitied her.

They said: *poor woman*.

Because they weren't perhaps really bad.

They weren't bad at heart.

They fulfilled the Scriptures.

What was curious about it was that everybody respected her.

Honored, respected, admired her grief.

Only a little did they push her aside, did they push her away.

With special attentions.

Because she was the mother of the condemned.

They thought: It's the family of the condemned.

They even said so in a low voice.

They said it among themselves.

With a secret admiration.

And they were right, it was all his family.

His family according to the flesh and his chosen family.

His family on earth and his family in heaven.

She followed, she wept.

Her eyes were so blurred that daylight would never seem bright to her.

Never again.

For the last three days people had been saying: She looks ten years older.

I just saw her.

I just saw her last week.

In three days she has put on ten years.

Never again.

She followed, she wept, she didn't quite understand.

But she understood very well that the government was against her boy.

And that is a very bad business.

That the government was putting him to death.

Always a very bad business.

And one which could not turn out well.

All the governments were together against him.

The government of the Jews and the government of the Romans.

The government of judges and the government of priests.

The government of soldiers and the government of parsons.

He would surely not get out of it.

Certainly not.

Everyone was against him.

Everyone was for his death.

For putting him to death.

Wanted his death.

Sometimes you had one government for you.

And another against you.

And so you could get out of it.

But he had all the governments against him.

All the governments to begin with.

Then the government and the people.

It was that which was strongest.

It was principally that which was against you.

The government and the people.

Who as a rule never agree.

And then you take advantage of that.

You are in a position to take advantage of it.

It very seldom happens that the government and the people agree.

And then he who is against the government.

Is with the people.

For the people.

And he who is against the people.

Is with the government.

For the government.

He who is backed by the government.

Is not backed by the people.

He who is upheld by the people.

Is not upheld by the government.

So leaning on one or the other.

On one against the other.

You could sometimes get out of it.

You might sometimes come to an agreement.

But they had no luck.

She saw very well that everyone was against him.

The government and the people.

Together.

And that they would get him.

That they would down him.

What was curious was that all derision was heaped on him.

Not at all on her.

For her.

There was no derision.
There was only respect for her.
For her grief.
For her woe.
They didn't insult her.
On the contrary.
People even refrained from looking at her too much.
All the better to respect her.
All the more to respect her.
She too had gone up.
Gone up with everybody else.
Up to the very top of the hill.
Without even being aware of it.
Her legs carried her and she did not even know it.
She too had made her way of the cross.
The fourteen stations.
As a matter of fact was it fourteen stations?
Were there really fourteen stations?
Were there really fourteen?
She didn't know for sure.
She didn't remember.
Yet she had made them.
She was sure of that.
But you can be mistaken.
In moments like that your head swims.
We who have not made them we know it.
She who had made them didn't know.
Everybody was against him.
Everybody wanted him to die.
It is curious.
People who are not usually together.
The government and the people.

So that the government bore him a grudge as did the
   rudest of carters.
As much as the rudest of carters.
And the rudest of carters like the government.
As much as the government.
That was awful luck.
When you have one for you and the other against you,
   you come through sometimes.
You get out of it.
You can get out of it.
You can come through.
But he would not come through.
Surely he would not come through.
When you have everyone against you.
But what had he done to everyone.

I am going to tell you:
He had saved the world.

She wept and wept.
For the last three days she had been weeping.
No, for the last two days only.
No, only since the day before.
He had been arrested the evening before.
Only.
She remembered well.
So.
How time flies.
How quickly time flies.
No, time passes slowly.
How slowly it passes.
She thought there had been three days.
What mistakes you can make.

He had been arrested in the garden of Olives.
Which was a place where people walked.
On Sundays.
He had been arrested the evening before in the garden
   of Olives.
She remembered well.
She remembered very well.
But it seemed to her.
She thought there had been three days.
At least.
And even more.
Much more.
Days and days.
And years.
It seemed to her it had almost always been.
Always so to speak.
It seemed to her.
It had always been like that.
In life there are things that happen that way.

Everyone was against him.
From Pontius Pilate to the last of carters.
She followed from afar.
Close up.
From somewhat afar.
Rather close up.
That howling mob.
That pack giving tongue.
And biting.
That howling mob that howled and hit.
Without putting their heart into it.
Putting their heart into it.

126

Because they were fulfilling the Scriptures.
You can say that they hit religiously.
Since they fulfilled the Scriptures.
Of the prophets.
Everyone was against him.
From Pontius Pilate.
That Pontius Pilate.
Pontius Pilatus.
Sub Pontio Pilato passus.
Et sepultus est.
A decent man.
At least they said he was a decent man.
Kind.
Not unkind.
A Roman.
Who understood the country's interests.
And who had a lot of trouble governing those Jews.
An intractable race.
But that's how it was, for the last three days a fit of
    madness had turned them against her boy.
A fit of madness. Something like hydrophobia.
Yes they were like mad dogs.
Against him.
What was the matter with them.
He hadn't done that much harm.
All of them.
And at the head of them Pontius Pilate.
The man who washed his hands.
The procurator.
The procurator for the Romans.
The procurator of Judea.
All of them. And Caiaphas the high priest.
The generals, the officers, the soldiers.

The noncommissioned officers, the officers commanding one hundred men, the centurions, the decurions.
The priests and the high priests.
The writers.
That is, the scribes.
The pharisees, the publicans, the toll collectors.
The Pharisees and the Sadducees.
The publicans who are you might say tax collectors.
And who are not worse than others for that reason.
It had been told her that he had disciples.
Apostles.
But you didn't see any around.
Perhaps it wasn't true.
Perhaps he didn't have any.
Perhaps he had never had any.
You make mistakes, sometimes, in life.
If he had had any, you would have seen them.
Because if he had had any, they would have showed up.
How's that? They were men, they would have showed up.

Not only did she weep and weep.
She wept for today and for tomorrow.
And for all her future.
For all her life to come.
But she wept, she wept also.
She wept for her past.
For all the days when she had been happy in her past.
The innocent woman.
To wash away the days when she had been happy in her past.

To wash away her days of happiness.
Her former days of happiness.
Because those days had deceived her.
Those deceitful days.
Those days had betrayed her.
Those days of long ago.
Those days when she should have wept in advance.
By way of storing up.
You should always weep by way of storing up.
Ahead of the days to come.
Of misfortunes to come.
Of misfortune on the lookout.
She should have taken precautions.
She should have foreseen.
You should always take precautions.

Had she known.

Had she known she would always have wept.
Wept all her life.
Wept in advance.
She would have suspected something.
She would have made the first move.
In that way she would not have been deceived.
She would not have been betrayed.

She had betrayed herself by not weeping.
She had robbed herself.
She had deceived herself.
By not weeping.
By accepting those days of happiness.

She had betrayed herself.
She had let herself be drawn into the game.

When you think that there had been days when she
    had laughed.
Innocently.
The innocent woman.
Everything went so well in those days.
She wept and wept to wash away those days.
She wept and wept, she washed away those days.
Those days she had stolen.
Which had been stolen from her.
Those days which she had filched from her poor son
    who at that moment was dying on the cross.

Not only did he have the people against him.
But two kinds of people.
Both kinds of people.
The poor people.
Who are serious.
And respectable.
And the poverty-stricken folk.
The down-and-out.
Who are not serious.
Nor respectable.
He had against him those who worked and those who
    did nothing.
Those who worked and those who didn't work.
Together.
At the same time.
The working people.
Who are serious.

And respectable.
And the beggar folk.
Who are not serious.
But who are perhaps respectable just the same.
Because you don't know.
You get bewildered.
You are no longer in your senses.
Your mind is deranged when you see such things.

He had the city workers against him.
Workers of the city.
Those who work in the city.
At their bosses' place.
At the bourgeois place.
And also, at the same time, together, the field workers.
At the same time also.
The peasants going to market.
Really he had done no harm to all those people.
To all those people there.
Really it goes too far.
They always go too far.
People are such mischief-makers.
They went too far.
Really he hadn't harmed everybody.
He was too young.
He hadn't had time.

To begin with he would not have had time.

When a man is down everyone falls on him.

You Christians know what he had done.

He had done this.
He had saved the world.

It is a singular lot to turn people about.
To turn everybody against you.
She wept and wept, and because of it she had grown
    ugly.
And the greatest Beauty in the world.
The mystical Rose.
The Tower of ivory.
Turris eburnea.
The Queen of beauty.
In three days had become dreadful to see.
People said that she had put on ten years.
They knew nothing about it. She had put on more
    than ten years.
She knew, she felt that she had put on more than ten
    years.
She had aged the space of her lifetime.
Fools.
By the space of her whole lifetime.
She had aged by her entire life and by more than her
    life, by more than a lifetime.
For she had grown older by an eternity.
She had aged by her eternity.
Which is the first eternity after God's eternity.
For she had aged by her eternity.

She had become Queen.
She had become the Queen of the Seven Sorrows.

She wept and wept, she had grown so ugly.

In three days.
She had become dreadful.
Dreadful to behold.
So ugly, so dreadful.
That they would have laughed at her.
Surely.
If she had not been the mother of the condemned.

She wept and wept. Her eyes, her poor eyes.
Her poor eyes were reddened with tears.
And never would see properly.
After.
Since.
Afterwards.
Nevermore.
From now on never would she see properly.
To work.
And yet she would have to work to earn her living.
Her poor living.
Work some more.
After as before.
Until she died.
Mend stockings, socks.
Joseph would go on wearing out his clothes.
In a word all a woman has to do in her household.
You have such a time making a living.

She wept, she had become dreadful.
Her eyelashes stuck together.
Her eyelids, the upper one and the nether one.
Swollen, bruised, tinged with blood.

Her cheeks devastated by grief.
Her furrowed cheeks.
Her cheeks all seamed.
Her tears had as it were ploughed her cheeks.
Tears on either side had worn a furrow in her cheeks.

Her eyes smarted and burned.
Never had anyone wept so much.
And yet it was a relief for her to weep.
Her skin smarted and burned.
And during that time, on the cross, his **Five Wounds**
    burned.
And he had fever.
She too had fever.
And thus shared his Passion.

She wept, she looked so strange, so dreadful.
So dreadful.
That you would certainly have laughed.
And you would have made fun of her.
Certainly.
Had she not been the mother of the condemned.
Even the street urchins looked away.
When they saw her.
Turned their heads away.
Turned their eyes away.
So as not to laugh.
So as not to laugh in her face.

And you never can tell, perhaps, too, so as not to cry.
It was lucky he knew that old Joseph of Arimathea.
A worthy man, that old one, without a doubt.
It was lucky too that that old man was willing to take
    an interest in him.
In his remains.
His mortal remains.
She thus would have a great solace.
The only one.
One only.
The last one.
The solace of his sepulture.
Of his burial and sepulture.

He would even be buried in a fine sepulchre.
In a new sepulchre.
Hewn out of the stone.
Out of the rock.
Out of the solid rock.
When all is told he would be buried in a handsome
    shroud.
A sheet.
For his last bed.
For his last sleep.
When all is told he would be buried in a rich man's
    sepulchre.

It was lucky that old man was going to look after him.
To take an interest in him.
In his body. In his remains.

His mortal remains.
You see, it is always a good thing to have influential
    friends.
That wise old man.
A worthy man.
Prudent like all old people.
Thrifty.
Careful.
Attentive.
Paying attention.
Full of fussy attentions.
Thrifty.
Economical.
Perhaps a little miserly, like many old people.
Because not much of life is left them.
And life is the first among blessings.
The greatest blessing.
Boaz was economical, wasn't he?

Economical, sparing of his blood.
Economical, sparing of his money.
And even sparing of his time.
Yet he had had a fine sepulchre made for himself.
A handsome tomb.
A handsome monument.
Hewn out of the stone, out of the rock.
Out of the solid rock.

He had spent a little money on his sepulchre.

To be comfortable.

And now he lent, he gave, he gave up his sepulchre to Jesus.

Well now, that showed that her son was not so forsaken as all that after all.

Since a rich man lent him his sepulchre.

To lend your sepulchre is perhaps the greatest sacrifice you can make for a man.

Particularly when you are old.

And had counted on resting in it peacefully.

And had had it built on purpose for that.

On purpose for yourself.

To rest in it peacefully.

That old man.

You must agree that that old man had made the greatest sacrifice you can make for Jesus Christ.

He was a well-connected man.

He knew the government.

The governor.

The procurator of Judea.

He knew Pilate very well.

He may even have been on very good terms with Pilate.

You don't know.

You never know.

He had all the more merit in looking after her son.

She wept and wept. She melted.

She melted into tears.

She swallowed back her tears with her saliva.
And at the same time, her throat was dry and burning.
With fever.
Her gullet was dry.
And burning.
Her head was filled with water.
And there was always some.
There was always some running out.
And at the same time her head felt dry, heavy, hot.
Weighty.
And her eyes smarted.
And her temples thumped.
Because she had wept so much.
And because she still wanted to weep.

She wept, she melted. Her heart melted.
Her body melted.
She melted with kindness.
With charity.
Only her head didn't melt.
She walked on as if against her will.
She no longer knew herself.
She no longer bore any grudge against anyone.
She melted with kindness.
With charity.
It was too great a misfortune.
Her sorrow was too great.
It was too great a sorrow.
You can't bear a grudge against the world for a mis-
    fortune that is greater than the world.
It was no longer any use bearing a grudge against the
    world.
A grudge against anyone.

138

She who in the old days would have defended her boy
    against wild animals.
When he was small.

Today she abandoned him to that crowd.
She let him go.
She let everything sink.
What can a woman do in a crowd.
I ask you.
She no longer knew herself.
She had changed a lot.
She was going to hear the cry.
The cry that never will be quenched in any night of
    any time.

It wasn't surprising that she no longer knew herself.
Because she wasn't the same.
Up to that day she had been the Queen of Beauty.
And she never again would be, she would never again
    become the Queen of Beauty except in heaven.
The day of her death and of her assumption.
Eternally.
But today she became the Queen of Mercy.
As she will be forever and ever.

Just the same she was pleased that that rich man had
    looked after her son.
A man with a fine reputation.
Highly thought of.
A tradesman of good standing.

Who had retired.

Retired from business.

And very likely he had been on good terms with her
son.

Because you don't give your sepulchre just like that
to someone with whom you are not on good terms.

Whom you don't even know.

That way, you plainly saw, you could not say that her
son was a tramp.

A vagrant. A vagabond.

As the chief priests had kept on repeating before the
tribunal.

Although she had to admit that for the last three years
he had not been seen at home.

And that he was always on the roads with people who
were not workers who worked.

But it wasn't her business to accuse him.

Sometimes you have trouble with children.

Ma'am.

That one had always given them satisfaction.

All the satisfactions you can ask for in life.

As long as he had been a boy.

As long as he had stayed at home.

Until the day, until the day when he had begun his
mission.

When he had begun to fulfil his mission.

But since he had begun his mission.

Begun to fulfil his mission.

140

Since he had left home.

He had been a source of worry to them.

It had to be said, he had never been but a source of worry to them.

Very often you have a lot of worry with children.

Very often you have a lot of trouble with children.

He who in the old days had given them such satisfaction.

He had given them in the old days nothing but satisfaction.

Sometimes you have a lot of trouble with children.

When they grow up.

She had told Joseph, to be sure.

That it would end badly.

They had been happy up to his thirtieth year.

It couldn't last.

It couldn't end well.

It couldn't end otherwise.

He drew after him.

He walked the roads.

He drew after him on the roads people she didn't want to malign.

But the proof that they weren't worth much.

Was that they had not defended him.

To begin with he made too many enemies for himself.

That was not prudent.

Enemies always turn up again.

141

Enemies you make for yourself always turn up again.
He disturbed too many people.
Also.
People don't like to be disturbed.

You are sometimes strangely rewarded in life.
Never had a child made his mother cry so much.
You sometimes have strange rewards.
You are sometimes often strangely rewarded in life.
Never had a boy made his mother cry so much.

As he her.
Those three days and those three nights.

Those three years.

What a pity. A life that had begun so well.
It was a pity. She well remembered.
How he beamed on the straw in that stable at Beth-
    lehem.
A star had risen.
The shepherds worshiped him.
The magi worshiped him.
The angels worshiped him.
What had become of all those people.

You are sometimes strangely rewarded.
With children.

A star had risen.
The shepherds worshiped him.

And offered him wool.
Fleeces.
Skeins of wool.
The kings worshiped him.
And offered him gold, incense and myrrh.
The angels worshiped him.
The wise kings Gaspar, Melchior and Balthasar.
What had become of all those people.

What had become of all that crowd.
Yet they were the same people.
The same crowd.
People were still people.
The world was still the world.
The world hadn't been changed.

Kings were still kings.
And shepherds still shepherds.
The great were still the great.
And small fry still small fry.

The rich were still the rich.
And the poor were still the poor.
The government was still the government.
She didn't see that as a matter of fact he had changed
    the world.

It was the same shepherds, the same peasants from the
    country.
Who had come to town.
Today.
Who were on his heels and shouted at him.

The world, then, had been changed in thirty years.
She didn't see.
That as a matter of fact he had changed the world.
That was after him howling for his death.
She did not see that as a matter of fact.
He had changed the world.

One man pulled at him, the other pushed him.
In one direction and in the other.
But they pulled him and pushed him.
Always in the direction of that hilltop Golgotha.
What a pity, it was a life that had so well begun.
Everybody had welcomed.
His coming into the world.
His birth.
Which is called his Nativity.
Had welcomed him so nicely.
When he was small.
But now he was grown up.
Now that he was a man.
Nobody would hear of him anymore.
Yet it was the same people.
And yet it was the same man.

Nobody would hear of him anymore.
All they wanted was to hit him, all of them.
With howls.
Dreadful howls.
And death cries.

They saw, they heard nothing else.

They felt nothing else.
Their one idea.
Their one and only idea.
Was to hit him.

When he was small, everybody had been well disposed
    towards him.
Everybody was glad to see him.
But now he was grown up.
And had become a man.
Nobody wanted him anymore.
They didn't even want to hear about him.
The world is fickle.

Yet there had been enough talk about him in the
    world since then.

Nobody wanted to see him.

The world has changed a great deal.
Men have changed a great deal.

Small children, small worries. Big children, big wor-
    ries.
You sometimes have trouble with children, ma'am.
You couldn't say that she had enjoyed the company
    of her son.
She who had been expecting so much.

She who had so very much congratulated herself
    about it.

You couldn't say that she had benefited much by it.
You couldn't say that.
But it may have been their fault too.

You never could tell.

It was their fault. It must have been their fault.
They had always been too proud of him.
Joseph and she, they had been too proud of him.
It was bound to end badly.
You mustn't be proud like that.
You mustn't be as proud as that.
You mustn't boast.

Weren't they pleased.
On the day when that old fellow Simeon.
Sang that hymn to the Lord.
Which will be sung forever and ever.
Amen.
And then there was that old woman in the temple.

Weren't they proud.

Too proud.

And that other time too.
The time when he shone among the doctors.
At first they got quite a jolt.
When they came home.

He wasn't there.
All of a sudden he wasn't there.
They thought they had forgotten him somewhere.
Mary was all taken aback.
They thought they had lost him.
At first they thought they had lost him.
That was no joke. It made her tremble yet.
It isn't something that happens every day to lose a
twelve-year-old boy.
A big twelve-year-old boy.

Fortunately they found him in the temple in the
midst of the doctors.
Sitting in the midst of the doctors.
And the doctors listened to him religiously.
He was teaching, at the age of twelve he was teaching
in the midst of the doctors.
How proud they had felt.

Too proud.

Just the same he should have been on his guard that
day.
He had really been too brilliant, he shone, he was
radiant, too much so, among the doctors.
Too much so for the doctors.
He was too great among the doctors.
For the doctors.
He had let it be seen too clearly.
He had let it be seen too much.

He had made it known too manifestly that he was
  God.
Doctors don't like that.

He should have been on his guard. Those people have
  good memories.
It is even because they have such good memories that
  they are doctors.
He had certainly hurt their feelings that day.
Doctors have good memories.
Doctors have memories that go way back.

He should have been on his guard. Those people have
  memories that go way back.
And then they always stick together.
They uphold each other.
Doctors have memories that go way back.
He had certainly hurt their feelings that day.
When he was twelve.
And when he was thirty-three they caught up with
  him.
And this time they wouldn't let him off.
It meant death.
They had him.
He was theirs to kill.
When he was thirty-three they caught up with him.
Doctors have memories that go way back.
They had caught up with him at the half-circle.
At the about turn.
At the turn of his bodily life.
At the turn of his mystical life.

148

And they had set him on his way to death.
To that death.

They had a firm hold on him.
This time.
And they would not let him go.
They would never let him go any more.
Ah he no longer shone among the doctors.
Seated among the doctors.
He did not shine.
And yet he shone forever.
More than he ever shone.
More than he ever shone anywhere.

And such was his reward.
You are sometimes strangely rewarded in life.
You sometimes get strange rewards.
And they got along so well together.
The boy and his mother.

They had been so happy in those days.
The mother and her boy.

Such was her reward.
Thus was she rewarded.

For having borne.
Given birth to.
Fed at the breast.
Carried.
In her arms.
Him who died for the sins of the world.

For having borne.
Given birth to.
Fed at the breast.
Carried.
In her arms.
Him who died for the salvation of the world.

For having borne.
Given birth to.
Fed at the breast.
Carried.
In her arms.
Him through whom the sins of the world will be for-
  given.

And for having cooked his soup and tucked him in
  bed until his thirtieth year.
For he willingly let her surround him with her love.
He knew all that wouldn't last forever.

And now she had seen him treated in a way that no
  mother would care to see her son treated. Maltreatments. Maltreatments. Blows. Unspeakable abuse.
  Insults. Maltreatments and the least said about
  them the better.

Unspeakable maltreatments.
And death to cap it all.
With death to cap it all.

You have such trouble with children.

150

You bring them up and afterwards.
She felt all that went on in his body.
Particularly his sufferings.
All that children give you is worry.
All that was in his body.
In her body as well as in his.
She felt her body as well as his.
Because of her motherhood.
She was a mother.
She was his mother.
His mother according to the works of the Spirit and
    his mother according to the flesh.
His foster mother.
He also had a cramp.
He had above all a cramp.
A dreadful cramp.
Because of that position.
Staying always in the same position.
She felt it.
Being compelled to stay in that awful position.
A cramp in his whole body.
And the whole weight of his body bore down on his
    four Wounds.
He had cramps.
She knew how much he suffered.
She well felt how much it hurt him.
She suffered in his head and in his side and in his four
    Wounds.[1]

---

[1] "She suffered in his head, etc." A reminiscence of Madame de Sévigné's celebrated statement in one of her letters to Madame de Grignan, her daughter: *"J'ai mal à votre poitrine."* "I have a pain in your chest."

And he said to himself: There is my mother. What
  have I made of her.
What have I made of my mother.
That poor old woman.
Who has become old.
Who has been following us for the last twenty-four
  hours.
From judgment hall to judgment hall.
And from judgment hall to public square.

Honor thy father and thy mother
That thy days may be long in the land.
It was the law of his father.
Our father who art in heaven.
As he had dictated it to Moses.
The first Lawgiver.
His father speaking in the Burning Bush.
And as for him, that was his way of living long in the
  land.

If not in his eternity.

And that was how he honored his father and mother.

If not in their eternity.

He had made of her that old woman.

It is the custom, when parents are old.
For children to feed their father and mother.

When father and mother have grown old.
It is the custom. And it is the law.
When the children have grown up.
When the children are big.
Are men.
It is the custom. It is the law. It is the rule.
The law of his father.
And as for him, that was how he fed his parents.

If not in his eternity.

He had caused his mother to make her stations of the
    cross.
From afar and close up.
From somewhat afar and somewhat close up.
She had followed.
She had made stations of the cross much more painful
    than his own.
For it is much more painful to see your son suffer.
Than to suffer yourself.
It is much more painful to see your son die.
Than to die yourself.

He had **fed them.**
Fed his parents.
But as far as he was concerned, it was with gall and
    bitterness he had fed them.

It is the custom, it is the law, it is the rule.
For sons to bring in something to their parents.
For **children.**

As they grow up.
To bring their parents something.
As they grow old.
As for him, that is what he had brought his father and
    mother.
That is what he had brought his mother.
What he had put in her hand.
That is how he had rewarded her.
He had brought her.
He had put in her hand.
The Seven Sorrows.
He had brought her.
He had put in her hand.
To be the Queen.
To be the Mother.
He had brought her.
To be.
Our Lady of Seven Sorrows.

It must be said too.
It must be said that it was a royal gift.
It must be said that it was an eternal gift.

And so like all the dying he went over his whole life
    in his mind.
All his life at Nazareth.
He saw himself all along his whole life.
And he wondered how he could have made so many
    enemies for himself.
It was like winning an impossible wager. How he had
    succeeded in making so many enemies for himself.
Like winning a wager. Like a challenge.

The men of the city, those of the suburbs and those
   of the country.
All those who were there, who had come.
Who had gathered there.
Who had assembled.
As for a holiday.
An odious holiday.
The day laborers, the odd job men.
The hirelings, the rentiers.
The high priest, the chief priests.
The writers, that is to say, the scribes.
The pharisees, the toll collectors.
The publicans who are the tax collectors.
The Pharisees and the Sadducees.

Christians, you know why:
It was because he had come to announce the reign
   of God.

And when all is told those people were right.
All those people were not so misled as all that.
It was the great holiday that was being held for the
   salvation of the world.

Only it was he who bore the costs.

In a way he could understand about those that bought
   and sold in the temple.
It was he who had begun.
He had been angry with them one day.
Angry with a holy anger.

And he had driven them out of the temple.
Striking them hard with a scourge.
Striking them hard, perhaps, with a scourge.
And with words no doubt unpleasant to their ears.

He had thus hampered them.
In their trade.
Disturbed them.
For a while.
In their dealings.
He had interfered with their interests.

He may well have hurt their business.

He had driven the dealers from the temple.
All those who sold and bought in the temple.
He had overturned the tables of the money-changers.
Mensas numerariorum.
And the seats of them that sold doves.
Et cathedras vendentium columbas.
And would not suffer that any man should carry any
    vessel through the temple.
*Et non sinebat ut quisquam transferret vas per tem-
    plum.*
But it was the fault of those dealers too.
Why had they made a den of thieves.
Of the house of God.
Is it not written.
Nonne scriptum est:
That my house shall be called by all nations the house
    of prayer.

*Quia domus mea, domus orationis vocabitur omnibus
    gentibus.*
But you have made of it a den of thieves.
Vos autem fecistis eam speluncam latronum.

And he continued to teach in the temple.
And to heal.
He taught every day in the temple.

That is what he had done in Jerusalem.
Almost immediately after he entered Jerusalem.
Almost immediately after he had entered Jerusalem.
Seated on the colt of an ass.

That the Scriptures of the Prophets.
Might be fulfilled.

Also he didn't care for tradespeople.
A workman.
Son of a workman.
Foster son.
Son raised.
By a family of workmen.
He instinctively disliked tradespeople.
He knew nothing about trade.
About business.
All he knew was to work.
He was inclined to believe that all tradespeople were
    thieves.

In a way, he understood about the dealers, the dealers
in the Temple.
But as for the others.
Like a dying man, like all the dying, he went over his
whole life.
As he was about to present it.
To bring it back to his father.
One day his comrades had found him too great.
Simply.
One day his friends, his friends had found him too
great.
One day the citizens had found him too great.

And he had not been a prophet in his own country.

Christians, you know why:
It is because he had come to announce the reign of
God.
Everybody had found him too great.
It was too obvious that he was the son of God.

When you frequented him.

The Jews had found him too great.
For a Jew.
Too great a Jew.
It was too obvious that he was the Messiah foretold
by the Prophets.
Announced, awaited for centuries and centuries.

He went over, he went over all the hours of his life.

All his life at Nazareth.
He had sown so much love.
He reaped so much hatred.
His heart burned within him.
His heart devoured with love.
And to his mother he had brought this.
To see treated in such a way.
The fruit of her womb.

And it was the same people who on Palm Sunday.
A few days before.
A few months, a few weeks.
Palm Sunday.
Had greeted him in triumph.
As he entered Jerusalem triumphantly.

His heart burned within him.
His heart was devoured within him.
His heart burning with love.
His heart devoured with love.
His heart consumed with love.
And no man had ever given rise to so much hatred.
And no man had ever given rise to hatred of such a
    kind.
It was like a wager.
It was like a challenge.

As he had sown so had he not reaped.
His father knew why.

Did his friends love him as much as his enemies hated
  him.
His father knew.
His disciples did not defend him so much as his ene-
  mies pursued him.
Did his disciples, his disciples love him as much as his
  enemies hated him.
His father knew.
His apostles did not defend him so much as his ene-
  mies pursued him.
Did his apostles, his apostles love him as much as his
  enemies hated him.
His father knew.
Did the eleven love him as much as the twelfth, as
  the thirteenth hated him.
Did the eleven love him as much as the twelfth, as
  the thirteenth had betrayed him.
His father knew.
His father knew.

What then was man.
That man.
Whom he had come to save.
Whose nature he had put on.
He did not know.
As man, he did not know.
Because no man knows man.
Because a man's life.
A human life, as man, is not sufficient to know man.
So great is he. And so small.
So high up. And so low.
What then was man.

That man.

Whose nature he had put on.

His father knew.

And those soldiers who had arrested him.

Who had taken him from judgment hall to judgment hall.

And from judgment hall to public square.

And those executioners who had crucified him.

People who went about their work.

Those soldiers who cast dice.

Who divided his clothes.

Who cast dice for his clothes.

Who drew lots for his robe.

They were those who even so bore no grudge against him.

That thirty years of hard work and three years of hard work.

That thirty years in retreat and three years in public.

Thirty years in his family and three years among the people.

Thirty years in the workshop and three years in public.

Three years of public life and thirty years of private life.

Had not crowned.

Thirty years of private life and three years of public life.

(He had put his private life before his public life.
His retreat before his preaching)
(Before his passion and his death)
Since it had yet needed the crowning of that death.

Since it needed the fulfilling of that martyrdom.

Since it needed the attestation of that testimony.

Since it needed the consummation of that martyrdom
   and of that death.

Since it needed, since it had needed the completion
   of that three day agony.

Since it needed the exhausting of that supreme agony
   and of that horrifying anguish.

And the descent from the cross, and the burial; the
   three days in the sepulture, the three days in the
   tomb, the three days in limbo, until the resurrection; and the strange post-mortem life, the pilgrims
   at Emmaus, the ascension on the fortieth day.

Since it had to be.

For the Son of God knew that the sufferings
Of the son of man are unable to save the damned.
And going mad with despond even more than they,
Dying Jesus wept over the forsaken.

162

Mad with the common despond.

Mad even more than they with *their* despond, with
the same despond as they, with their own despond.
He shared with them the same despair. But he was
God: how great a despair his must have been.

As he felt his human death rising up towards him,
Out of his sight was his tearful and sorrowing mother,
Standing below, erect at the foot of the cross, out of
his sight John and Magdalen.
And dying Jesus wept over the death of Judas.
Dying his death, only our human death, he wept over
that eternal death.

He the first among saints over the first among the
damned;
He the greatest of saints over the greatest of the
damned;
He the author, the inventor of redemption,
Over the first object of damnation.
He the author, the inventor of the redeeming of our
souls;

He the inaugurator of salvation,
Over the inaugurator of perdition.

Over the first object of reprobation.
Eternal reprobation.

For he knew that the supreme reprobate
Had thrown away the money of the blood for which
   he had been payed.
The price of blood, the thirty pieces of silver in the
   money of that country;

Counted in pieces of silver, in pieces of silver of that
   time and of that country.

The thirty pieces of silver, a temporal price, a temporal money, temporal pieces of silver.
Those wretched thirty pieces of silver, price of eternal
   blood;

Those wretched thirty pieces of silver, it would have
   been better not to mint them.
Never to mint them.
Woe to him who struck them.
   In the effigy of Caesar.
Woe to him who received them.
   In the effigy of Caesar.
Woe to all of those who had anything to do with them.
   In the effigy of Caesar.
Woe to all of those who traded with them.
   In the effigy, in the effigy of Caesar.
Who passed them to each other from hand to hand.
Dangerous pieces of silver.
More counterfeit.
Infinitely more dangerous.
Infinitely more counterfeit than counterfeit money.
And yet they were genuine.
Those pieces of silver that will be talked about in all
   times. And more than in time.

Beyond time.

The very priests who had given them.

Would no longer accept them.

The priests, those who offered up sacrifices, the elders
who had given them.

To pay for innocent blood.

Refused to take them back.

Then Judas.

Which had betrayed him.

Had given him up.

When he saw that he was condemned.

Repented himself.

And driven by regret, by remorse, by repentance.

Brought again the thirty pieces of silver.

To the chief priests.

And elders.

Saying:

*I have sinned in that I have betrayed the innocent
blood.*

And they said:

What is that to us?

See thou to that.

And he cast down the pieces of silver in the temple.

And departed.

And went and hanged himself.

Hanged himself.

And the chief priests.

Took the silver pieces.

And said.

It is not lawful for to put them into the treasury.

The sacred treasury.

Because it is the price of blood.

And they took counsel.
And bought with them the potter's field.
To bury strangers in.

Wherefore that field was called.
Aceldama.
That is to say.
The field of blood.
Unto this day.

Then was fulfilled that which was spoken by Jeremy
  the prophet.
Saying.
And they took the thirty pieces of silver, the price of
  him that was valued.
Whom they of the children of Israel did value.

And gave them for the potter's field.
As the Lord appointed me.

(For he knew) that the most forsaken of all men was
  hanging himself over there.
Somewhere, under a fig tree of that country.
And that the money was used for the potter's field.

All the past was present to him. All the present was
  to him present.
All the future, all the time to come was present to
  him. All eternity was present to him.
Together and separately.

166

He saw everything in advance and everything at
the same time.
He saw everything afterwards.
He saw everything beforehand.
He saw everything as it happened, he saw everything
at that moment.
Everything was present to him in all eternity.

He knew about the money and the potter's field.
The thirty pieces of silver.
As he was the Son of God, Jesus knew all.
And the Saviour knew that, even though he gave
himself up completely,
He was not saving that Judas, whom he loves.

And it was then he knew infinite suffering,
It was then he knew, it was then he learned,
It was then he felt the infinite agony,
And cried out like a madman in his horrifying an-
guish,
With a cry that caused Mary, who yet stood, to stag-
ger.

And by the Father's mercy he died his human death.

Why, sister, should you want to save from eternal hell
the dead who are damned, should you want to save
better than Jesus the Saviour?

JEANNETTE

(Stops spinning.)

So then, Madame Gervaise, who must be saved?
How must one save?

MADAME GERVAISE

How you do talk, child, how you do talk. We are
behind Jesus, child, we walk behind him, we are the
flock of his disciples. We must receive his teachings.
We are the flock that walks behind the shepherd. We
are not to run, we are not to walk ahead of him.

We are his flock of pupils. We are the flock. We
must walk behind the shepherd. We are not to run
ahead. Like sheep with the staggers. We are not to
get in the way of his feet. We are not to get in his way.

As he walks.

JEANNETTE

I ask you, Madame Gervaise: who then must be
be saved? How must one save?

MADAME GERVAISE

By imitating Jesus; by listening to Jesus.

(A pause.)

The master saviour did not even try to save the
damned, *afterwards,* because he knew that eternal hell
is hopelessly closed in.

He knew that they were precluded souls, souls de-
clared precluded.

(A pause.)

The master saviour did not sow nor did he want

others to sow, for he knew how to multiply loaves; we must not sow, for he still knows how to multiply loaves.

Nemo potest. No man can *serve two masters: for either he will hate the one, and love the other; or else he will hold to the one, and despise the other. Ye cannot serve God and mammon.*

Therefore I say unto you, Take no thought for your life, what ye shall eat . . . ; nor yet for your body, what ye shall put on. Is not the life more than meat, and the body than raiment?

Behold the fowls of the air: for they sow not, neither do they reap, nor gather into barns; yet your heavenly father feedeth them. Are ye not much better than they?

Which of you by taking thought can add one cubit unto his stature?

And why take ye thought for raiment? Consider the lilies of the field, how they grow; they toil not, neither do they spin:

And yet I say unto you, That even Solomon in all his glory was not arrayed like one of these.

Wherefore, if God so clothe the grass of the field, which today is, and tomorrow is cast into the oven, shall he not much more clothe you, O ye of little faith?

Therefore take no thought, saying, What shall we eat? or, What shall we drink? or, Wherewithal shall we be clothed?

For after all these things do the Gentiles seek: for your heavenly father knoweth that ye have need of all these things.

But seek ye first the kingdom of God and his righte-
ousness; and all these things shall be added unto you.

Take therefore no thought for the morrow: for the
morrow shall take thought for the things of itself.
Sufficient unto the day is the evil thereof.

Malitia sua: its woe, its malice, its evil; its work;
its trial; alas perhaps its temptation; perhaps its sin.

(A brief pause.)

The master saviour did not want Peter to draw his
sword against the soldiers in arms: we mustn't go to
war.

Et ecce unus. And, behold, one *of them which were*
with Jesus stretched out his hand, and drew his
sword . . .

JEANNETTE

So they had swords.

MADAME GERVAISE

They therefore had swords. *Drew his sword, and*
struck a servant of the high priest, and smote off his
ear.

Then said Jesus unto him, Put up again thy sword
into his place: for all they that take the sword shall
perish with the sword.

Thinkest thou that I cannot now pray to my
father, and he shall presently give me more than
twelve legions of angels?

But how then shall the Scriptures be fulfilled that
thus it must be?

In that same hour said Jesus to the multitudes, Are
ye come out as against a thief with swords and staves

for to take me? I sat daily with you teaching in the
temple, and ye laid no hold on me.

But all this was done that the Scriptures of the
prophets might be fulfilled.

JEANNETTE

Then all the disciples forsook him, and fled.

MADAME GERVAISE

Child, child, how you do talk, you do not talk like
a little girl.

JEANNETTE

I believe . . . I believe.

MADAME GERVAISE

Daughter, child, what dare you say?

JEANNETTE

I believe that, had I been there, I would not have
forsaken him.

MADAME GERVAISE

Daughter, child, let us keep ourselves from the sin
of pride. We are made as others. We are Christians
like others. We would have been like them. We would
have been among them. We would have acted like
them. The Scriptures had to be fulfilled. All forsook
him. Not one remained. It had to be. All forsook him.
We too would have forsaken him.

If we had been with them, if we had been among
them, if we had been of them, from among them, if
we had been they, we would have done as they did.
How can you think, why do you think that we would
not have done as they did.

We are no better than the others.

171

JEANNETTE

They weren't French. They weren't French knights.

MADAME GERVAISE

Daughter, child, how you do talk. You don't talk like the others, you don't talk like everyone else.

JEANNETTE

Frenchmen would never have forsaken him.

MADAME GERVAISE

Daughter, child, how you do talk. You don't talk like a good Christian, like an ordinary Christian.

JEANNETTE

French knights, French peasants, people from our country would never have forsaken him.

People from the country of France. People from the country of Lorraine.

MADAME GERVAISE

Daughter, child, let us not think proud thoughts, let us keep ourselves from the sin of pride. Those men you talk about so lightly were the first Christians.

JEANNETTE

They were happy once.

MADAME GERVAISE

They were the first Christians. It wasn't easy to be the first Christians.

JEANNETTE

They were happy.

MADAME GERVAISE

It wasn't easy. The whole earth, the earth was all besmeared with paganism. The whole earth was a slave to the worship of false gods. They were the first Christians of Christendom. Their business was to wash the face of the earth, of all the earth, like a dirty child's.

They were the first Christians of Christendom. After Jesus, the inventors of Christendom.

JEANNETTE

They were happy. Never would our Frenchmen have thus forsaken him, never would our Frenchmen have forsaken him.

People from the country of Lorraine, people from the country of France.

MADAME GERVAISE

Daughter, child, how you do talk. You don't talk as you should. They were the first saints of Christianity; they were the first Christians of Christendom; they were the first saints of Christendom, the founders, *(Jeannette moves)* after Jesus, *(bolder)* with Jesus the founder of Christendom, the authors, the second authors, the authors of Christendom, the inaugurators of Christendom, the founders, the authors, the inaugurators, the inventors of all Christendom.

After God, with God, if it please God the creators of all Christendom.

JEANNETTE

Never would the people of these parts have forsaken him.

The Scriptures had to be fulfilled. Let us not speak
lightly, child, daughter, do not speak without due con-
sideration of those old saints, of the first saints. They
were the first patrons, our first patrons. They were
the teachers and harbingers of the others, of all those
who came after. Of us ingrates. Those who made
ready the lodging. The lodging of the perishable
earth. The eternal, perishable, imperishable lodging
of the perishable earth. They made lodgings, they
made the lodging, the billeting, they made ready the
lodgings for others. For all the others. And therefore
for us. For us among the others. For us ingrates. They
had names. They were the first disciples, they were
the twelve apostles. The old saints, the eternal saints,
the first old saints. The eternal old saints. They had
names that count, child. They did not bear names of
day before yesterday. Of the thirteenth and four-
teenth centuries. They began everything. After Jesus.
With Jesus. The old saints eternal. They bore names
that will resound forever. They bore, they inaugurated the names that thousands and thousands and
hundreds of thousands of Christians took on since,
have since taken on, to have them as patrons; and
among those thousands and thousands, right in the
midst of those thousands and thousands and those
hundreds of thousands of Christians, saints themselves, who took on the same name, saints in their
turn, thousands and thousands of saints who having
taken on the same name, they too, in order to have a
patron, they themselves following them, themselves
became patrons, in their turn they themselves patrons,

sanctified the name anew, clothed it with a new glory, over the ancient glory, like a long file, like a spiritual band, like an eternal family, temporal, eternal, behind the file-leader, like a particular family, a particular spiritual family, a spiritual temporal eternal family, behind the particular father of the family, head of the family, behind the initial patron, behind the first patron; who thus doubled, tripled the name, who doubled and tripled its holiness, who doubled and tripled its glory, who doubled and tripled its patronage, who made the patronage twofold, threefold, fourfold, fivefold, sixfold, tenfold, hundredfold. That is how it is, child. Such were the names they bore. That is the way it is managed. They were the saints of the saints, of those who later became saints. They were the patrons of the patrons, of those who later became patrons. They were the first-day saints.

They did not bear names of today or of yesterday.

JEANNETTE

They were happy once.

MADAME GERVAISE

They bore, they upheld the first names in the world, they upheld, they put forward, they started, they invented the first names in Christendom. Child, child, they invented Christendom itself; after Jesus, with Jesus they upheld, they put forward, they started, they invented Christendom. Now that is done, there is nothing complicated about it, it is easy to speak lightly of them, it is done forever, done for eternity, done by them and impossible to undo. Done by them for us. When we do it, child, it is done. But when they did it, it hadn't been done. They, child, had to wash the world's face, the whole world's, they had to wash the face of the earth.

The face of the earth.

They promoted the first names in the world. They promoted Christendom itself.

JEANNETTE

They were happy once.

MADAME GERVAISE

They upheld great names. Those were great names, child, those names you lightly mention, they were sacred names. They were the first of Christians. They were the first of saints. Their names were the first among names. They were the first of Christian names. They were the Christian name itself. After Jesus, with Jesus they imagined, they upheld, they invented, they bore, they introduced, they put forward, they started being holy, being Christian in very sooth, bearing the Christian name. They made the beginning. They began being Christian. They began being holy. They were the initial men, the initial saints, the initial Christians, the initiators of everything.

We people come after, we follow in their train. It is not the same thing.

It isn't the same.

We follow in their train.

Christians and successors.

Sons and successors.

Sons in spirit and successors in spirit.

Spiritual sons and spiritual successors.

JEANNETTE

They were happy once.

MADAME GERVAISE

Where there was nothing, they did everything. **And** where there is everything, we hardly do anything at all. They had names which were taken, which will forever be taken as coverings; as a covering of patronage; names that were especially taken, which were excellently taken and will forever be taken by the saints, their successors.

And where there is everything, what there is, we lose.

JEANNETTE

They were happy once.

MADAME GERVAISE

They were therefore somewhat like Jesus. They were the saints of the saints, of the other saints, of the saints their successors, of the lineage of the other saints their successors. They were the patrons of the patrons, of the patrons their successors, of the lineage of the other patrons their successors. They were therefore somewhat like Jesus. Jesus was the saint of all the saints, the patron of all the patrons, the saint, the patron of all Christendom. What Jesus was for everyone, for all Christendom, for themselves, and for all the other saints, for themselves and for all the other Christians, for all those of Christianity and all those of Christendom, for all those of the communion, they themselves were that in their turn, by the organization of patronage, by a delegation, by a distribution, through a sharing, through a communication, through an allotment, through a carrying forward, through a real imitation of Jesus, they themselves were that for their particular families; for their particular lineage, for their spiritual lineage, in the great Christian family, in the great common family, in the great family of the communion. A kind of eternal redistribution had been performed ahead of time for their glory. And in the particular family of each one, in the spiritual family, in each particular family there have been great saints.

By a dividing up, by a repercussion of holiness; by a redistribution, by a reversal of patronage.

JEANNETTE

They were happy once.

MADAME GERVAISE

It was *James* and John, sons of Zebedee. Those names which you lightly mention, child, they called themselves two brothers, *Simon called Peter, and Andrew his brother, casting a net into the sea: for they were fishers.*

And he saith unto them, Follow me, and I will make you fishers of men.

And they straightway left their nets, and followed him.

And going on from thence, he saw other two brethren, James the son of Zebedee, and John his brother, in a ship with Zebedee their father, mending their nets; and he called them.

And they immediately left the ship and their father, and followed him.

JEANNETTE

They were happy once.

178

They inaugurated the city of God, the kingdom of God on earth. Thy kingdom come. The reign of God on earth. For the saints their successors. For the Christians, for all the Christians their successors. For us. The wages they had so hardly earned. The souls of the sinners he had redeemed. They were named, wasn't there one who was named Zachariah; they were named *the first, Simon, called Peter,* Simon, surnamed Peter, *and Andrew his brother;*

James the son of Zebedee, and John his brother; Philip and Bartholomew; Thomas, and Matthew the publican; there were some of different trades; *James the son of Alpheus, and Thaddeus;*

Simon the Canaanite . . .

JEANNETTE

and Judas Iscariot who also betrayed him.

MADAME GERVAISE

Unhappy, unhappy child. But one of them received his name from the very hands of Jesus, from his own hands.

JEANNETTE

That very man who denied him. People from this country would never have denied him.

MADAME GERVAISE

Unhappy, unhappy child, what is going on at the back of your mind? *Et ne nos inducas in tentationem.* Let us keep ourselves, child, let us keep ourselves from the sin of pride, let us keep ourselves from the temptation of pride. He received his name from the very hands of Jesus Christ. It was a fine name baptism, child. Jesus Christ was his godfather and his godmother. That man of whom you so lightly speak, that Christian, that saint, *primus,* the first of all, he not only had what we have had: the baptism of water. He not only had what we have not: the baptism of blood. He also had, in addition, the baptism of name. It was Jesus Christ who gave him his name. What a name. His eternal name for the Church's eternity. He received his name, his new name, his real name, his only name, from the own hands, from the very hands of Jesus.

The first Pontiff. The first Roman.

The holder of the Keys.

The first bishop of Rome.

His invented name; his new name; his created name.

Jesus saith unto them, But whom say ye that I am?

And Simon Peter answered and said unto him, Thou art the Christ, the Son of the living God.

And Jesus answered and said unto him, Blessed art thou, Simon Bar-jona, for flesh and blood hath not revealed it unto thee, but my father which is in heaven.

And I say also unto thee, Thou art Peter, and upon this rock I will build my church; and the gates of hell shall not prevail against it.

And I will give unto thee the keys of the kingdom of heaven.

Thrice. The same man. The same man denied him thrice.

MADAME GERVAISE
(As in righteous wrath:)

Peter's denial, Peter's denial. That is all you have to say, Peter's denial. *(Stammering, almost spluttering. With anger.)* That is what we allege, that denial, we say that to screen, to hide, to excuse our own denials. In order that our own denials be forgotten, that we forget them ourselves, that we succeed in making ourselves forget them. To talk about something else. To change the conversation. Peter denied him thrice. What then? As for us, we have denied him hundreds and thousands of times for the sake of sin, for the strayings of sin, by the denials of sin.

Tu es Petrus, he alone received his name thus, directly, from the own hands of God, he alone after Jesus. But Jesus said *tu* in speaking to him.

The sweeper saints, the great sweeper saints of the world.

JEANNETTE

Never would the men of this country, never would the saints of this country, never would even simple Christians of our regions have forsaken him. Never would French knights; never would French peasants; never would simple parishioners of French parishes. Never would the men of the crusades have forsaken him. Never would those men have denied him. You would sooner have wrenched their heads off.

People of the country of Lorraine. People of the country of France.

The prophecies had to be fulfilled.

JEANNETTE

They would have let others fulfil them. Never would the king of France have forsaken him. Never would Charlemagne and Roland, never would the people around here have allowed that to be done. Never would the workmen of the cities, never would the workmen of the market towns have allowed that to be done. The farrier would have taken his hammer. The women, the poor women, the gleaners would have taken billhooks. Never would Charlemagne and Roland, the men of the crusades, my Lord Godefroy de Bouillon, never would Saint Louis and even the Lord of Joinville have forsaken him. Never would our Frenchmen have renounced him. Saint Louis, king of France, Saint Louis of the French. Never would Saint Denis and Saint Martin, Saint Genevieve and Saint Aignan, never would Saint Loup, never would Saint Ouen have forsaken him. Never would our saints have renounced him. They were saints who weren't afraid.

MADAME GERVAISE

Child, child, how you do talk. You rely on the second saints against the first saints; you make a decision in favor of the second saints against the first saints; you call the second saints to witness against the first saints. How impious, child. You bring division in the Church, you bring a debate into the communion of saints. A division, a debate in the communion.

You call forth the second Christians against the first

Christians, the second saints against the first saints.
A house divided against itself shall perish.

JEANNETTE

I say what I believe. I know what race the people
around here belong to.

MADAME GERVAISE

You bring division in the Church that is one, that
Our Lord founded one, that he wished to be one, that
he will eternally keep one. You bring division, you
bring a debate into the communion that is one.

JEANNETTE

I say how we are, and how our saints were. They
weren't afraid of blows.

MADAME GERVAISE

There is only one holiness. They are the same
saints. There is only one holiness, which comes from
Jesus.
Which is the holiness itself of Jesus.
Eternally poured out again.

JEANNETTE

Sainte Genevieve, Saint Aignan, Saint Loup were
not afraid of meeting the heathen armies. They
weren't afraid of the heathen armies. And Saint Martin was a soldier. It wasn't a little band of Roman soldiers and of Roman executioners. It was no longer a
few decurions. And their little decury, their wretched
little decuries. That had to be put to flight. It was
no longer a question but of a few centurions. Of some
centurions and of the third or fourth part of their
centuria. They rushed ahead with a firm heart to

meet innumerable armies, heathen armies. They didn't lower their eyes, those didn't. They didn't tremble in all their limbs. They did not deny. They did not renounce. And Saint Bernard who preached the second crusade. He too was a second saint. They bore the body of Jesus to meet innumerable armies. And Saint Genevieve was a poor woman, a little girl of Paris. And they were innumerable armies, heathen armies full of murder and blood. And there wasn't a sword, there was no longer a sword, there was no longer a question of a sword, like the sword of the high priest's soldier servant. Like the sword or the staff of that Malchus. Of a sword, of a policeman's sabre. A rural policeman's sabre. There were thousands and thousands and hundreds of thousands of sabres. And they had been used. And were still used. A lot of them. For a long time.

That knew how to do service.

That were ready to do service.

They went to it nevertheless. In the folds of their cloaks they bore the glory of God.

They were shepherds. They did more for their flock than the others had done for the great Shepherd, for the shepherd in chief. They did more for God's people than the others had done for God himself.

MADAME GERVAISE

All the saints have always borne the glory of God in the folds of all their cloaks.

JEANNETTE

They were barbarians, barbarian armies, innumerable armies, heathen armies. One hundred times more barbaric, one hundred times worse, infinitely more

184

barbaric, infinitely worse than the English themselves. And than the Burgundians.

They went to it nevertheless. In the folds of their cloaks, they bore the glory of God and the body of Jesus. And the barbarian heads bowed before them. Conquerors in defeat, they conquered, they triumphed over the conquerors themselves.

MADAME GERVAISE

All holiness comes from God, all holiness proceeds from God. There is only one holiness, which comes from Jesus Christ. All the saints are God's saints, the brothers of Jesus, the brothers in holiness of Our Lord Jesus Christ himself. The young brothers, the little brothers, the younger brothers of Jesus. There is only one holiness, it is the holiness of Jesus himself. All holiness is the same. All holiness comes from God, who is the everlasting fount of holiness. All holiness proceeds from Jesus who is its fount and first author. And the original object of holiness as well as its original residence. The original seat, the seat, everlasting. Who is the first example of holiness. The model, the inventor, the object of all imitation. The happy issue, the greatest, and the first, the first realization. All the saints in the world are but the reflection of Jesus. All holiness in the world is but the reflection of the holiness of Jesus.

JEANNETTE

Saint Francis would not have renounced him.

MADAME GERVAISE

You bring in a debate where there must never be

185

a debate. You bring in division where never in eternity there will be any division . . .

For the Church is imperishable; the communion is imperishable and *a house divided against itself shall not stand.*

JEANNETTE

Saint Clare would never have renounced him.

MADAME GERVAISE

The Church is one; the communion is one; one in time; one in eternity.

JEANNETTE

Renounced, renounced, that is worse than everything. Madame Colette would never have renounced him.

MADAME GERVAISE
(Anger welling up in her.)

But really now, really, those saints you call to witness against the first saints, those Christians you trot out against the first Christians, from Charlemagne to Saint Francis and to our Saint Clare, those saints, those Christians whom you turn against themselves by turning them against others, they weren't of your opinion. They did not turn against their brothers. They didn't turn against their elders. They didn't turn against those who preceded them. They didn't turn against the eternal fount.

Against their models, against their examples, against the object of their imitation.

JEANNETTE

I say things as they are.

MADAME GERVAISE

They had the greatest devotion, they had nothing but devotion for the saints their brothers, for their brothers who came before them. They timidly and humbly intended, they intended only to imitate them. All together; all together like themselves; all together after them; all together with them; to imitate Jesus.

They had but devotion and imitation for their brothers; for their elder brothers; for their big brothers.

JEANNETTE

I can't lie. I don't want to lie. I say things as they are.

MADAME GERVAISE

They judged, those did; they knew that they belonged to the same body; to the same body of Christendom. They knew that they stuck together, that they were all in one block, of the great block of Christendom.

That they were all in one block, in the only block, the same block, the great block of holiness.

Participating in the great block of holiness.

JEANNETTE

To renounce, never, to renounce. How could they renounce the Son of God.

MADAME GERVAISE

Jews, Greeks, Latins, Frenchmen, there are not several kinds, there are not four races of saints. Jewish saints, Greek saints, Latin and Roman saints, French saints; English saints and Burgundian saints,

187

there is only one race of saints which is the eternal race. There is only one race of saints which is the race that will not end; the spiritual race; the eternal race; which will never end, never in eternity. For it proceeds, for it comes from the fount that will never run dry in all eternity.

All those saints that you call to witness, those great saints, Charlemagne and Saint Louis, Saint Genevieve and Saint Francis, from Charlemagne to Saint Francis, I not only say that they would never have talked thus, that they would never have talked like you. I say that they would not have heard except with horror the words which you have just spoken. Against such words they would have protested, they would have risen, they would have risen up, with all their might, with all their feeble might, their victorious might. Against the evil use to which they were being put. Against the pernicious use. Against that impious use, rousing them against their brothers, using them against their predecessors, against their founders, against the first drinkers at the eternal fount, against the first who were nourished at the imperishable fount.

JEANNETTE

All I say is this: as for us, we would never have forsaken him.

MADAME GERVAISE

We forsake him every day, wretched girl, we forsake him every day. You call on Saint Francis, my poor child. Through Madame Colette, through Saint Clare, by the spiritual filiation of Saint Clare, spiritual daughter, spiritual sister, spiritual godchild, spiritual companion, I have put myself under the rule of Saint Francis; of the same saint, of that saint you call upon; I have bound myself, eternally have I bound myself, eternally in all eternity, I have bound myself to the rule of Saint Francis; I have taken refuge under the rule of Saint Francis; eternally in all eternity I have taken shelter under the rule of Saint Francis. Of the same saint you pit against me. I will live and die, if it please God, if God be willing, I will live and die under the rule, in the rule of Saint Francis. That is why you call on Saint Francis for me. You are not stupid. You are not silly. You pit my master against me. You pit my patron against me. You pit my saint against me. You pit my master against me.

You pit my father against me.

(A pause.)

Well, I who belong to Saint Francis to you who don't . . .

JEANNETTE
(sharply:)

to me who belong to nothing. Gently, Madam. One is always from somewhere, one always belongs to something and to someone in Christendom.

There are no tatterdemalions and ne'er-do-wells in Christendom. There are no tramps, no vagrants.

You who belong to Saint Francis to me who belong to Saint Remy, and Saint John and Saint Joan. To Saint Remy for my parish; and to Saint John and Saint Joan for my baptism, for the baptism of my name, for the sponsorship of my baptism. To Saint Remy as parishioner. And to Saint John and Saint

Joan as Christian, as one baptized, as baptized Christian. Saint Remy the patron, the great patron of my parish. And Saint John and Saint Joan my patrons, my great patrons.

The great patrons of my baptism.

My baptism patrons and my patrons from heaven.

But the great patron is Jesus, our patron, our great patron, everybody's great patron.

And the Holy Virgin is our mother.

You who belong to Saint Francis; to me who belong to Saint Remy, and to Saint John and to Saint Joan.

You who belong to Jesus; to me who belong to Jesus.

MADAME GERVAISE

I who belong to Saint Francis; to you who belong to Saint Remy, and to Saint John and to Saint Joan.

I who belong to Jesus; to you who belong to Jesus, I say:

I say: if my master were here, my patron and my father; and I say if your patrons were here, your fathers and godfathers, your spiritual godfathers; if Francis were here, my father, my master Francis; and if Saint Remy, and Saint John and Saint Joan were here, I tell you, daughter, you would sing small. You wouldn't be so proud, child; you wouldn't be so haughty. For they were great saints. All bowed before them. You take advantage of the fact that I am only a poor woman, a poor sinner, alas, like everyone else. A sinner. A poor woman. A woman poor in grace. And you too would have bowed before them. To-gether with me, together with everybody, we would

190

have bowed before them. Together all in a heap, together in common, together in communion. They were so close to grace, they were so full of the fount, they were so close to the fount, they were so full of grace that grace ran out of them, ran visibly out of them, overflowed from them as from a spring of running water. And not only, child, did everyone obey, did everyone follow; did everyone bow; not only that; but everyone was happy; everyone rejoiced in them, everyone rejoiced because of them; everyone fed on them; everyone was happy to obey, happy to follow, happy to yield, happy to bow the head. You would have bowed, child, you would have inclined your head. Everyone obeyed, followed joyfully. It was not like today, all astringency and ingratitude, rigor and hardness, it wasn't only constraint and forcing. It was an inexhaustible joy, a perpetual blessing, a joy, the sweet joy of following, contentment in going ahead. It would have been necessary to make an effort, on the contrary, in order not to go ahead, a thankless effort, an impossible effort, an effort, too, which no one made, which you did not have the courage to make. A joy of plentifulness and benediction. You were like a piece of land lit by the sun, warmed by the sun, watered by the good tepid rains of springs, the good tepid rains of autumn. You gave up. You melted. And you felt free, you felt that you were free. You were full of joy, do you understand. You cried for joy. You would have had what was coming to you. You cried for joy. You gave up. You cried for grace. Everybody. You drank that milk. You took in fresh supplies, you became satiated, you bathed in that grace.

There was too much of it. Some of it was lost. Too much has been lost. You no longer knew what to do with it. It ran in all directions. It is no longer that way nowadays. Nowadays we lack it. Nowadays we canalize it. Nowadays we are like farmers, like peasants, like ploughmen, like gardeners who lack water; so we make dams in order to lose nothing of that thin trickle; in order not to lose anything. We make dams, and canals, and canalizations; we organize, *we make regular,* we utilize that thin trickle of water; of an eternal water; of the water, of a water from an eternal spring. We utilize it to the utmost, as much as we can. And our lands remain meagerly watered. Our lands remain meager. A meager trickle of water. Meager lands. Meager crops. With our meager arms we will bring in nothing but meager crops. Happy will we be if we bring in any. A river ran. An inexhaustible river ran. There is a difference between a great river and children's games. Between a great river and canals, artificial canals, water games. But as for me, I am but a poor woman. So you take advantage of it. You take an unfair advantage of it. You are stronger than I. But God is stronger than you and I. You resist. You argue. You rebel. But God, if it please God, is stronger than any one. God, if it be his will, will perhaps do what unworthy I cannot do. The merits and the prayers of Jesus, the promises of Jesus, the merits and the prayers of all the saints work for us. And who knows, very small though I be, though unworthy, though infirm, God will perhaps grant my prayers something. He will perhaps grant, he will no doubt grant yours a great deal, for you must pray for yourself, you must begin by praying for yourself. God

192

likes you to pray and to begin by praying for yourself. Otherwise, there would be pride. There is pride, the fact is there is a touch of pride. God will tear you away, God will free you from that bondage. God will save you, God will calm that unrest in you. That dangerous, that perilous unrest. At the peril of your soul. That mortal unrest. God will enlighten you in that darkness, that shadow in which you are seeking.

We must pray for ourselves in others, among others, in the communion of all.

All I want to say to you, all I can say to you, I, poor woman, is that if the great Saint Francis were here, *our brother Francis,* I not only say that he would not talk like you, child, daughter; I say that he would not have heard such words except with horror; I say that they would have broken his heart. Or rather, no, poor child. *(Almost laughing.)* They would have had no effect on him. Because he would not have heard anything at all *(laughing)* , and not because he is deaf, he would not have heard them at all. And they would have been spared everybody, they would have been spared the face of heaven. For had he been present, child, had our brother Francis been here, were he here, poor child, dear child, you would indeed not have spoken them, he being present, you would have lowered your brow, my fine child, you heart would have melted. And you would have followed, you would have followed. Your heart would have melted in true piety. God, your saints should always remain alive. They go too soon; always too soon. You always call them back too soon. You have enough of them for yourself. You have enough of them in your house. And we haven't enough of them. We people haven't enough of them. They fail us. They fail us so very much. We never have enough of them. They succeeded. But as for us, we are poor women who do not succeed.

I will go further, daughter, *and if it be possible to experience grief in heaven,* words like the ones you have just, you had just spoken, are what can hurt the most, if they hear them, if they ever hear them, what can most hurt the saints who are in heaven.

JEANNETTE

I just said, forgive me, I just say: never would we have forsaken him, never would we have renounced him. That is the truth. I just say: never would the people around here, never would we, never would people from Lorraine, never would people from the valley of the Meuse, never would the parishioners of our parishes, never would those of Vaucouleurs, never would those of Domremy, never would those of Maxey, never would we have forsaken him. We are great criminals, we are great sinners. But we would not have done that.

Never would we have allowed that to be done.

Which is worse.

Which is the worst.

Of all.

I don't like the English. I say: never would the English have allowed that to be done.

MADAME GERVAISE

Be careful, child, pride is watching, and the evil one never slumbers. His greatest masterpiece is to divert toward sin the very feelings which were driving us to God, which were casting us toward God.

Which were leading us, which were putting us in God's service.

We have two kinds of feelings, child. Two breeds of feeling grow in us, wax in us, child, divide our soul, two breeds of passion: two slopes of inclined planes draw us along; two sets of machinery make us lean forward, incline us; two mechanisms, two slopes of inclined planes draw us along; two sets of dipping machinery, two inclinations make us slide, make us fall on one or the other side.

There are feelings which incline us, which lead us to God, which take us, which bring us back to God; there are passions which cast us toward God; there are mechanisms, sets of mechanism which push us toward God; there is the slope, the inclined plane, the inclination, the leaning which makes us slide, which makes us fall on God's side.

And unfortunately, alas, alas, there is the other side. There are the feelings which draw us away, which lead us away, which lure us away, which turn us away from God; which unlead us, which unbring us, which unbring us back, which lure us away from God; there are the passions which tear us away from God; there are the mechanisms, the sets of mechanism which draw us away from God; there is the slope, the inclined plane which makes us skid away from God; the inclination, the leaning which makes us slip, which makes us fall on the side, alas, other than God's side.

But really, as long as the devil is at work for his part, my poor child my poor child you can almost say that there is nothing to say; alas alas, unfortunately alas, it is a sad thing to say, a dreadful thing to say:

but really, when he is at work for his part, you could almost say, you understand what I mean, my little child, in a way you could almost say that he is in his right; that it is legitimate, legitimate so to speak; when he is at work in his province, in his kingdom, alas in his kingdom of perdition; when he is at work in feelings that work for him; when he is at work in feelings that serve him, that are useful to him, naturally; that are made, alas, that are so to speak made for him; when he is at work, when he is at play with passions to his liking; when he plays at his game, the wretch; when he goes down the slopes that are, alas, so to speak reserved for him.

So to speak abandoned.

Only, then his province was always limited, his kingdom, his wretched kingdom. He never obtained, he could obtain only a certain number of souls. So he invented, wretch that he is, he imagined, the perfidious, the pernicious, the pestilential one that he is, invented, had the idea of inventing a sin; a new sin; a singular sin; a sin proper; a particular sin; a sin by which he would at last pass over to the other side; by which he thus would double, would infinitely enlarge his province, his kingdom of perdition; by which at last he would touch, he would tempt the very saints of God.

He would reach with the hand the very saints of God.

Wretch, twofold wretch, wretch by one and the other hand.

A sin that is no longer like all the others. Like the other sins. Like all the world of sins. Like the sins its brothers, its wretched brothers. A new sin. A cleverly invented sin. A sin apart from other sins. From all other sins. A sin that makes virtues and vices play together, virtues as well as vices. And even more, and perhaps better, virtues certainly better than vices. That reigns first of all over the other sins its brothers, its little brothers, its shameful brothers, its brothers of perdition. That reigns so to speak equally over virtues. That gathers, that unites in a low, in a shameful bondage, that utilizes, that equalizes in a common, in a shameful equality virtues and vices.

That plays equally one and the other game.

Old pride is watching, child. Be careful, be careful, old pride is watching.

The first, the oldest master of the world. The oldest master of bondage. The first one that was invented. The oldest one that was invented. Pride that lost the angels themselves.

The master that plays one and the other game. That gives and takes with one and the other hand. That puts in both hands. That plays both games.

Old pride never rests. Be careful, be careful, child, old pride never sleeps.

Old pride does not know slumber by night. Old pride knows no bed of rest.

It is the evil one's greatest invention, child, poor child. You would almost admire, so to speak, you understand, you see what I mean, child, you understand how I say that, you see what I mean when I say

197

that. It is really his masterpiece, you could say that it is almost a masterpiece. For thus he tempted, he was able to tempt, he succeeded in tempting the very saints of God. And all the strength that nature had given us, he turns it around for us, it is that strength which he turns for us against nature and against God: and all the strength that the grace of God gives us, he turns around for us, it is that very strength which he turns for us against God. It is an admirable canalization, you see what I mean, an unbelievable turning aside, a turning, a reversal of canalization, a prodigious tapping. Ah yes, ah yes, it is a masterpiece. How could God allow him to invent that. By that ministry, by that means, by that canalization. By the ministry of this means, by this canalization. It is dreadful. Really it is dreadful when you think of it. So the feelings which turned us Godward, it is by them, by those very feelings that he turns us away from God. The feelings that led us naturally toward God, which put us on our way to God, which made us end in God, it is by those feelings that he draws us away from him. The passions, the floods of passion that cast us in God, it is by them that he tears us away from him. And the floods of grace, unhappy child, the floods of God's grace, it is in those floods, in those very floods that he drowns us in sin. That is how he works, child, that is what pride is. The evil one is always the evil one. He plays his game inside God's game, in God's very game. And all that God has given us to help us find salvation, Jesus himself and the merits, Jesus and the promises, he uses all that to undo us, he makes it all work for our undoing, he makes it work for our everlasting perdition.

198

He plays on the side where he shouldn't play, where he never should have played, in God's game with God's game.

He makes use of everything, he turns everything around, he knows how to turn everything around. Jesus himself and the story of Jesus.

JEANNETTE

I just say: Frenchmen, Englishmen, Burgundians, never would my father, never would my mother, never would we have given him up; my father, that big strong man; my mother who went on pilgrimages; never would my uncle Lassois, my uncle Durand Lassois; never would my godfather, never my godmother; never my three brothers, never my big sister; never would the curé himself, the curé of Domremy, old Father Bardet, who is nevertheless such a good sort of man, such a kind man; and so meek, so peaceable, *blessed are the peacemakers;* a man who would never get angry, a man who would never raise his voice on one occasion more than on another; a man who never does, who never did anyone any harm; and so much of a curé. Well, Monsieur le Curé would have lost his temper that day. Never would my uncle, never Hauviette, never Mengette, never would we have stood that. Our saints were saints who weren't afraid of blows.

MADAME GERVAISE

Old pride is always watching. When the devil works through the other sins, through the six capital sins, he plies his trade, the wretch; he plies his trade, he is at work in his profession. But when he works through pride, Lord, when he treads his way, when he goes ahead along the roads of pride, when he walks along those roads; along those byroads, those diverting roads; those roads that turn back; those roads of reversal; when he takes the cloak of pride, no, Lord, no, he overdoes it then. You let him do more than his business.

JEANNETTE

I just say: We would not have put up with that. We would not have stood that. We would not have allowed that to be done. I say: Hauviette. I say: Mengette, *(looking her suddenly in the eye.)* I say: You, Madame Gervaise, you would not have allowed that to be done.

MADAME GERVAISE

(Staggering all of a sudden under this thrust, under this invasion, under this onslaught; this direct onslaught; under this revelation of the most secret thought. She trembles. She suddenly blushes. Her eyes flash. Then she talks to reassure herself. Slowly, modestly, she quenches all that.)

Child, child, spare me.
He came during the night, like a thief, and made away with everything.

(Stuttering, stammering, gradually recovering possession of herself:)

I did not come into the world at that time, child.

JEANNETTE
(Implacably:)

You, you would not have renounced him.

MADAME GERVAISE

*(In an incredible effort, a terrible effort to be humble;
voluntarily, with a will to be humble; as if she were
cornered; shivering, trembling; closing her eyes;
humbly; she will end her speech in a colorless voice.)*

Child, I am like everyone.

I am no better than other people.

I did not come into the world at that time. God
makes us come into the world when he chooses. He is
always right. What God does he does well.

He came during the night like a thief; and he took
away everything.

JEANNETTE

(She manages to say with humility what follows:)

As for me, I am sure that I would not have abandoned him. God is witness that I would not have
abandoned him.

MADAME GERVAISE

*(Recovering by degrees her self-assurance, somewhat
through force of habit:)*

Desertion, desertion . . .

(Still perturbed:)

Old pride is watching. God causes us to be born
when he chooses. Old pride is not dead. Old pride
never dies.

Desertion, desertion, that is all you have to say; the
disciples' desertion, the apostles' revocation, the rene-
gading, the denial of Peter, that is all you have to say.
In the life of a whole saint, you take, you remember
this: that one day he was a renegade. It is easy now
to be a Christian, it is easy to be a parishioner. It was

not so easy when they began. You try to be smart, now, you try to be proud, you try to be strong, you try to be great. You try to be saints. It is easy now to be a parishioner. It was not so easy when there were no parishes and when the whole earth was un-ploughed. Thirteen centuries of Christians, thirteen centuries of saints have washed the face of the earth for you; thirteen centuries of Christians, thirteen centuries of saints have undeceived the earth for you; thirteen centuries have ploughed the earth for you. Ingrates, ungrateful people: Thirteen centuries have Christianized you, thirteen centuries of saints have sanctified the earth for you. And so, that is all you find to say. Thirteen centuries of Christians, thirteen centuries of saints have built your parishes for you, have wiped the earth for you, the face of the earth, have built your churches for you. And so, that is all you have to say. Ingrates, ungrateful people. When you came into the world, you found the house built and the table set. The Lord's table. And what you say is that one day, a day of mourning, the day of eternal mourning, is that one day he was a renegade.

The earth, the face of the earth was so dirty, child. All besmirched with dirt, all besmirched, all dirty with paganism.

All besmirched with the adoration of false gods.

With the worship of false gods.

And there wasn't a parish in the face of heaven.

Renegade, renegade. That's soon said. He once denied Jesus,—three times. And we, we, how many times have we denied him. Peter's denial, Peter's denial: what about your denial, your own denial. Our denial, my denial. Everybody's denial, the denial of all of you, of all of us everybody. Thousands and thousands of times do we deny him. And with a worse denial. Hundreds and thousands of times we forsake him, we betray him, we deny him, we renounce him. With what a renouncing. With a renouncing infinitely worse. For there is a difference. They were poor people who knew nothing, they were. They had not been asked anything. They had not been asked for their opinion. Jesus had gone by and taken them away. One day he had gone by like a thief. He had made away with everyone. He had taken everything, made away with everything. With all those who were marked. With all those who happened to be there. Who were at the customs. They were poor fishermen; of the sea of Tiberias. Which was also called the sea of Galilee. And those two who mended their nets with their father. And one day, in the stupor of that lightning event, in the trembling of that extraordinary revelation, one day, the poor people, yes, that's how it is, they missed their chance. They were in a fog that day. That was because they weren't trained, they weren't used to such a great event. They weren't used to it, they weren't in the habit of their own greatness. They were in no wise prepared for it. By all their former life. By their parents, by their trade, by their family. By their habits, by their friends, by their companions. By their conversations, by their everyday pursuits. They weren't warned. They didn't think, they didn't know that they had come into the world for that. On purpose for that, just for that. They didn't know their greatness, their own greatness, their vocation, the destination of their greatness. They hadn't been warned. They had received no warning. In a word, they were surprised. Naturally. They didn't expect it. You can understand that. It was the first time. But as for us.

(She speaks colorless words.)

Pride is watching.

Old pride is watching.

Child, we didn't come into this world at that time.

We are all of us like everyone else.

The earth was all dirty, all muddy, all besmeared with mire.

At that time.

In illo tempore.

In those days.

In diebus autem illis.

All miry.

And as for us the face of the earth had been washed for us, the plaster had been dried for us before we occupied the house, stocks were laid up and made ready for us from which we will take in fresh supplies forever.

JEANNETTE

I just say: I'm like everyone; (but) I know that I would not have abandoned him.

MADAME GERVAISE

They had no suspicion of their history, their own history, the greatness of their history. How would they have guessed it. Never had the like of it been seen. But as for us. As for us, we have been given thirteen centuries of warning. We have been given thirteen centuries of admonishment. Haven't we been sufficiently warned, though. We have thirteen cen-

turies of exercise. Thirteen centuries of existence.
We even have thirteen centuries of habit. We know.
We are informed. We shouldn't be surprised.

Haven't we been given enough warning though.
Thirteen centuries of Christians, thirteen centuries
of saints, thirteen centuries of Christendom. We
should know. Once. Once, twice, thrice. And the
cock crew. But as far as we are concerned it is the
thousandth, it is the hundred thousandth, it is the
hundredth of thousandth time that we give him up;
that we abandon him, that we betray him; that we
renounce him, that we deny him. Ungrateful people,
ungrateful people, but also renegade. Thousands and
hundreds of thousands of times we deny him for the
strayings of sin. How many times, thousands and hundreds of thousands of times the cocks in the farms, of
all the farms have crowed after we had denied him
thrice; upon our single, upon our double, upon our
triple denials. The cocks in the straw. On the manure
heaps in the farms.

Funny; they're always talking about that cock, he
is famous, about the cock that happened to be there
to crow over, to sound, to record Peter's denial. It's to
change, to turn the conversation. It's to sidetrack people. There have been cocks since. There are cocks in
our countries. And they are not idle. We do not allow
them to be idle. You would think that there were no
cocks in our countries. They never mention the cocks
in our countries. Alas alas there is not a cock in not
a farm that has not crowed over, that has not sounded,
that has not heralded forth to the rising sun, that has
not recorded, every day, at each sunrise, worse de-

nials. Denials that were more than triple. That has
not proclaimed man's shamefulness. The cock crows
at break of day. What the cock crows over at break
of day, at the break of every day; standing up straight
on the manure heaps of all the farms; standing up
straight with their spurs out, what they brag about,
what they celebrate, what they proclaim, what they
herald forth, is our untold denials. How can one hear
the crowing of the cock in the morning, how can one
hear the cock crow, a cock crow, in the morning, and
they begin again every day, and how many times each
day, how many times a day, without immediately
thinking of the threefold denial, without immediately
weeping over the threefold denial, and over our denials, which are more than threefold. Each day.

A cock crew for Peter; how many cocks crow for
us; the breed is not extinct.

The breed of cocks is not extinct.

Only we don't hear those, we don't wish to hear
them.

Alas, alas, he must be getting used to it. We have
given him the habit; given a habit even to him; we
have accustomed him to it. We have given him that
singular habit: of being denied.

We have made him acquire that habit.

The same event is always taking place. Through the
real presence, the presence of Jesus, the same event
is always taking place.

But those saints of whom you speak so lightly; and
not only you; everybody, everywhere, speaks lightly
of them; that Peter, our founder, of whom you speak

so lightly; who is always being made fun of by everybody; the master of the keys. They were the invested apostles. They were the first disciples.

Jesus forgave, and instantly, in advance he had forgiven Peter's denial. God send that he has acquired the habit; and that he likewise forgives us our countless denials.

God send that God has acquired the habit. May it be God's will to have acquired the habit. That habit too.

That habit like the other one.
Like the other one which we made him acquire.
That habit and not only the other one.

Peter our rock. Peter the rock of our foundation.

They were the first. They were the disciples. They were the apostles. They were the martyrs. Peter won the supreme honor of being crucified. Crucified like Jesus! What a sign. What an honor; a unique honor. What a sign of his destination. He was crucified head-down only, in a spirit of humility, because naturally no one can be crucified exactly like Jesus.

Jesus was the head and he the base. Jesus was the head and he the feet. The foot.

And Andrew, his brother Andrew was crucified on a Saint Andrew's cross.

When we have like them, as much as them, paid for our denials, our own denials, then, child, we can talk. When we have had that honor, when we have died for him, like them, then, child, we may perhaps be allowed to put in a word; we may have our say. (*Laughing almost inwardly.*) But then, child, it is then we shall say nothing. For then it is that we would have nothing to say. For it would mean that we were in the kingdom. In the kingdom where one says nothing more, where one has nothing more to say. For it would mean that we shared with them everlasting bliss.

It would mean that we shared their everlasting bliss.

Their bliss. The bliss they have won. In the kingdom where one says nothing more, because one has nothing more to say.

Because there is nothing more to say.

Jesus preached; Jesus prayed; Jesus suffered. We must imitate him just as far as our strength allows. Oh, we are unable to preach divinely; we are unable to pray divinely; and we will never have infinite suffering. But we must try with all our human might to say, to transmit as best we can the divine word; we must try with all our human might to pray as best we can according to the divine word; we must try with all our human might to suffer as best we can, and up to the extreme limit of suffering without ever killing ourselves, (to suffer) all we can of human suffering. That is what we must do here below, if we really don't want to let others lose their souls through our own cowardice, if we don't want to thus lose our souls with theirs through our own cowardice.

JEANNETTE

Just the same, I really think that at heart I am not a coward.

208

That is what we must do here below. For there are treasures. Just as there is unfortunately, so to speak, a sort of treasure of sins, fortunately, fortunately, there are other treasures.

There is in heaven, in heaven and on earth, in heaven and from thence on the earth, there is in heaven a treasure of grace; a treasure of graces; an eternal spring of grace; it is ever flowing and ever as full; it flows everlastingly and is everlastingly full: that is what the doctors on earth have not understood.

It is always full. It is always everlastingly full. That is what the doctors on earth have not understood.

There is a treasure of sufferings, an eternal treasure of sufferings. The passion of Jesus filled it up all at once; filled it completely; filled it infinitely; filled it for all eternity. And yet he is always waiting for us to fill it, that is what the doctors on earth have not understood.

There is a treasure of prayers, an eternal treasure of prayers. The prayer of Jesus filled it up all at once; filled it completely; filled it infinitely; filled it for all eternity; the time when he invented the Our Father; that time, that first time; that only time; the first time the Our Father came forth into the world; the time, the only time, the first time the Our Father appeared on the face of the world; uttered by those divine lips; shed light on the face of the earth; passing such lips;

the prayer that was to be said so many times afterwards, forever afterwards; to sound so many times on unworthy lips; the prayer that was to be repeated so many times; to sound so many times on human lips; afterwards for ever so many times; the prayer that was to sound so many times, to tremble so many times on sinful lips; to rise so many times to faithful lips. To sing so many times; to murmur. To tremble so many times in the choirs of the faithful, in the secret region of their hearts.

When prayer came forth that time, for the first time, the prayer which we shall never do more than echo.

The first time the Our Father came forth on the face of the earth, came forth into creation, shed light on the face of the earth; came from him.

Came forth on the face of the earth, shed light on the face of the earth.

The first time the Our Father went up to Our Father, who art in heaven.

Invented, uttered by his divine lips.

There is a treasure of prayers. Jesus, that time, all at once, that first time Jesus filled it up; filled it completely; for eternally. And he is still waiting for us to fill it, that is what the doctors of the earth have not understood.

There is a treasure of merits. It is full, it is completely full of the merits of Jesus Christ. It is infinitely full, full for ever in eternity. There is almost too much of it; so to speak; considering our unworthiness. It is crammed full. It is running over. Brimming

over; running over. It is infinite and yet we can add
to it, that is what the doctors of the earth have not
understood. It is full and is waiting for us to fill it up.
It is infinite and is waiting for us to fill it up. It is
infinite and is waiting for us to add to it.

He hopes that we will add to it.

That is what we must do here below. Happy
enough when the good Lord, in his infinite mercy, is
willing to accept our works, our prayers and our sufferings as a means of saving one soul. One soul, one
single soul is of an infinite price.

JEANNETTE

What then would be the price of a whole people of
souls; what then would be the price of an infinite
number of souls.

MADAME GERVAISE

There is a treasure of promises. All at once, straight
away, Jesus kept all the promises. He came and kept
all the promises. He kept all of God's promises, all
of the prophets' promises. All of God's promises
brought back to memory, reiterated by the prophets,
by the line of prophets. All the promises made to his
people, to the people of Israel; and in Israel to all
humanity. Singular promises. They were all fulfilled
at the first stroke, they were all crowned at one stroke.
And it will eternally be of us, it will also be of us, it
will finally be of us that they will await their fulfillment, that they will await their crowning. Singular
promises. Still singular. Doubly singular. It was to us
they were made. It was to us they were promised. And

when all is said it is on us that their fulfillment depends, it is by us that they expect to be crowned. It is in our hands, in our feeble hands, in our thin hands, in our unworthy hands, in our sinful hands that their very fulfillment lies together with the promise of their crowning. It is the world upside down. The one to whom the promise is made is also the one who, when all is said, keeps the promise, keeps the promise to himself. It is the world wrong side up. He who keeps the promise is the same as he to whom the promise is made. It is we who keep our word to ourselves. That is what the doctors of the earth have not understood.

JEANNETTE

One soul, one single soul is of an infinite price. What would be the price of a countless number of souls?

MADAME GERVAISE

You compel me. You are beyond me. When one says to save a soul, it means to save that soul, one is thinking of that soul; of the salvation of that soul. One says: to save a soul. It doesn't mean that one shuts out the others, that one thinks, that one works against the others, apart from the others; that one takes a stand against the others, apart from the others; that one prays apart from the others.

That would be praying outside the communion.

When one says to save a soul, one says, one means a soul, a certain soul. One doesn't say *one* soul, one only as when one counts *one, two, three.*

One never prays apart from anyone.

So as to keep anyone apart.

One never prays against anyone.

One says to save a soul, one puts it like that.

JEANNETTE
(As though she didn't hear:)

What will be the price of numberless souls?

MADAME GERVAISE

We must think of all, we must pray for all. And we should feel unduly happy when, by an infinite favor, he chooses that soul among those we have loved. Ah! Jeannette, if you knew . . .

(A brief pause.)

They have often told you, no doubt, that I had fled the world and that I had been cowardly, that I was cowardly, that I had left Mamma; that is all they have to say, that one flees the world, that we flee the world: if you knew through how many tears, through how much blood of my body and blood of my soul I have tried to save that soul! Forgive me, Lord, forever my pride in daring to choose the soul I wanted to save.

(A long pause.)

When the soul has come up before the Tribunal, if God has condemned it to eternal Hell, our works are of no avail for it; it is dead; our prayers are of no avail for it; for it our sufferings are of no avail. Let us not give for it, let us not give in vain for it our living works, our living prayers, our living sufferings: let the dead bury the dead.

JEANNETTE
(She stops spinning to enter into the argument.)

So then, Madame Gervaise, when we see a soul going to perdition . . .

MADAME GERVAISE
(With extreme though muffled violence; like a cry from under:)

Never do we know if a soul is going to perdition.

JEANNETTE

Alas! We well know that there are some who go to perdition. We well know. Come on, Madame Gervaise! We often think that such and such a soul is damned.

MADAME GERVAISE

Sister, when I believe that a soul has gone to perdition, I am unhappy and I offer to God this new suffering which closes around my soul, this suffering which is caused by the thought of a soul that is damned, although it still be here.

You offer God what you have. You offer God what you can.

JEANNETTE

And when you see that your prayers are in vain, Madame Gervaise, what then?

MADAME GERVAISE
(Very sharply; like a smothered cry; like a secret cry.)

We never know when a prayer is in vain.

(Blushing and quickly correcting herself:)

Or rather we know that a prayer is never in vain. There is the treasure of prayers. Since Jesus said his Our Father. Since the first time that Jesus said his Our Father.

(Very firmly.)

And even if it were so, it is the good Lord's business: our souls are his. When I have said my prayers and well borne my sufferings, he grants my wish: it is not for us, nor for anyone to call him to account.

JEANNETTE

What about suffering?

MADAME GERVAISE

He answers suffering as he answers prayer.

JEANNETTE

And when we see that Christendom itself, that all of Christendom gradually and deliberately sinks, sinks regularly into perdition.

MADAME GERVAISE

We shall see, we shall see, child. How much of it do you see. What do you know about it. What do you know. What do we know about it. We'll see what there is to see. We must let God's will come along and take its course. The world is going to perdition, the world is sinking into perdition. Since when are you aware of it, do you see it? Let us say eight years. Since when, to your hearing, do the older folk talk about it? Let us say forty, fifty years. Let us say from father to son since fifty or one hundred years. And then what? What are forty, what are fifty and one hundred years compared with what has been promised to the Church. And even if it had been going on for thirteen centuries. What are centuries of days and centuries of years. What are centuries of minutes. There will be centuries of centuries. We belong to the Church eternal. We are in Christendom eternal. We belong to Christendom eternal. These times have come, there will be other times. These times have come, there will be, there is eternity. What is the weight of centuries of centuries in the face of eternity.

Of real, of true eternity.

In the face of eternal promises. Of the promise of eternity. Of the promise made to the Church.

In the face of the promises.

In the face of promises weighed by events; poor miserable events; all that happens.

What do we know.

What do we see.

And even if it were so, it concerns the good Lord: Christendom itself is his, the Church is his. When I have said my prayers properly and properly borne my sufferings, he fulfils my wish according to his will: it isn't for us, it isn't for anyone to ask him the reason why.

We are in God's hand.

The ways of God are unfathomable.

JEANNETTE
(Somewhat sharply.)

Farewell, Madame Gervaise.

MADAME GERVAISE

Farewell, daughter. May Jesus the Saviour save your soul forever.

JEANNETTE

Amen, Madame Gervaise.

(She resumes her spinning.)

Orléans, who are in the country of the Loire.

(Madame Gervaise had left. But she returns before there has been time to lower the curtain.)